APOCALYPSE NOW

Francis Ford Coppola

AUTHORED by A. Boghani
UPDATED AND REVISED by Christine McKeever

COVER DESIGN by Table XI Partners LLC
COVER PHOTO by Olivia Verma and © 2005 GradeSaver, LLC

BOOK DESIGN by Table XI Partners LLC

Published by GradeSaver LLC, www.gradesaver.com

First published in the United States of America by GradeSaver LLC. 2013

ISBN 978-1-60259-402-9

Printed in the United States of America

For other products and additional information please visit
http://www.gradesaver.com

Table of Contents

Table of Contents

Biography of Coppola, Francis Ford (1939-)

Francis Ford Coppola is one of the most critically acclaimed and groundbreaking film directors of all time, whose work changed the face of American cinema. He was born on April 7, 1939 in Detroit, Michigan to Carmine Coppola and his wife, Italia. He was the second of their two sons, 5 years younger than his brother, August. Younger sister Talia was born in 1946. Both of Coppola's grandfathers immigrated to the United States from Italy, and the family "cherished their Italian origins," although they also learned to embrace everything America had to offer. Carmine and Italia moved around within the borough of Queens in New York City. Francis was not a strong student and in 1949, he contracted polio, which left him bedridden for 9 months. During this time, young Francis kept himself amused by experimenting with an 8mm film projector, puppets, and his family's television set. He started making home movies and later, after he was able to walk again, charged his friends money to see them.

Following in the footsteps of his elder brother, Francis attended Hofstra University in New York (where he met aspiring actor James Caan). He studied theater, and his plays were well-received by his classmates. After graduating in 1960, Francis went on to attend UCLA's film school with the goal of becoming a director in Hollywood. He met producer Roger Corman when the legendary B-Movie producer called UCLA looking for eager students to assist him. After being Corman's gopher for several months, Corman allowed Francis to make a film called *Dementia 13*, which he and several of his classmates shot in Ireland over 9 days. During the shoot, Coppola fell in love with Eleanor Neil, to whom he is still married. In 1963, Eleanor gave birth to their first child, Gian-carlo ("Gio"). Another son, Roman, followed in 1965.

Coppola showed early talent as a screenwriter, and soon Seven Arts, a well-regarded independent production company, offered him a contract. When Seven Arts partnered with Warner Bros., Coppola immediately sprung into action. He self-financed the development of *You're a Big Boy Now* and negotiated with Warner-Seven Arts to back his efforts. The film, which served as Coppola's UCLA thesis, was an official selection at the 1967 Cannes Film Festival. Coppola was only 27 years old. Next, Coppola was offered a job directing *Finian's Rainbow*, a Fred Astaire musical. He was fond of the Broadway show, as was his father. However, the film was a box-office disappointment - and according to Fred Astaire, his worst film. However, it was on the set of *Finian's Rainbow* that Coppola met his future friend and business partner - a young man named George Lucas.

Coppola made his next film, *Rain People* (1969) starring Robert Duvall, James Caan, and Shirley Knight with support from Warner-Seven Arts. Later that year, Coppola, along with George Lucas and legendary sound editor Walter Murch, started American Zoetrope in San Francisco. The company was founded "with the utopian vision of creating personal, artistic films" (Jones 18). They got a $600,000 loan from Warner Bros., but their first film, *THX 1138*, directed by George Lucas, was a disaster. Warner Bros got nervous about their investment in Zoetrope and asked for their money back. It was in this state of financial desperation that Francis Ford Coppola agreed to meet with Peter Bart about directing *The Godfather*.

Mario Puzo had set up the project at Paramount while he was still working on *The Godfather* novel. By the time Coppola signed on to direct the project, Puzo's novel was a massive hit, doubling the pressure on the untested, relatively new director to deliver. While *The Godfather* was in production, Coppola won an Oscar for *Patton* (1971), which he had co-written in 1966. In addition, his daughter Sofia was born in 1971.

Despite being plagued by on-set and budgetary tensions, *The Godfather* became the first film to ever earn $1 million per day at the box office during its 3-month run. It won three Academy awards in 1972, including Best Picture, and made Francis Ford Coppola a star.

After the success of *The Godfather*, Coppola produced *American Graffiti*, directed by his friend George Lucas - which was also a resounding success. Meanwhile, Paramount wanted to capitalize on the success of *The Godfather* and commissioned Coppola to direct a sequel, giving him double the budget. *The Godfather Part II* won three Academy Awards, including Best Picture (the first sequel ever to do so) as well as Best Adapted Screenplay and Best Director. Coppola is one of the few directors to ever be nominated twice in the Best Director Category - in 1974, he was also nominated for his work on *The Conversation*.

Coppola managed to make *The Conversation* in between the two *Godfather* films. Starring Gene Hackman, it was released in 1974. Although Coppola had started developing the idea in 1966, his recent successes allowed him the opportunity to finally put the film into motion. *The Conversation*, which deals with technology and espionage, was released while America was reeling from the Watergate scandal, although Coppola denies any connection. Besides its three Academy Award nominations, the film won the Palme d'Or at the 1974 Cannes Film Festival. In 1975, Coppola bought a vineyard in Napa Valley, California, which he still runs.

Coppola's tremendous success certainly did not hamper the ambitious young man's hunger for a challenge. His next film, *Apocalypse Now*, would be the most difficult (and some would argue, the most brilliant) film of his career. It is based on a screenplay by George Lucas and John Milius about the Vietnam War. It shares moral and thematic elements with Joseph Conrad's *Heart of Darkness*, which had never been successfully adapted to the screen. (Note: Orson Welles had worked on a film version of *Heart of Darkness* for years, but was unable to crack it). *Apocalypse Now* took Coppola three years to complete, during which he had to contend with a cataclysmic typhoon, his main actor having a heart attack, negotiations with Filipino army helicopters, and the near dissolution of his marriage. However, despite all the troubles, *Apocalypse Now* was a massive success. Coppola won his second Palme d'Or for the film, which grossed $78 million at the box office.

Coppola decided then to re-open Zoetrope and try once again to make a musical - *One from the Heart.* It was an ambitious flop, thus ending Coppola's box-office streak. His next two films, adaptations of S.E. Hinton's novels *The Outsiders* (1982) and *Rumble Fish* (1983), though critically acclaimed, did not have the same financial success as Coppola's previous outings. Robert Evans then hired Coppola to direct *The Cotton Club* from a screenplay by Mario Puzo, hoping that the *Godfather* dream team would prove to be a winning formula, but he was wrong. The film was a disaster. Coppola was forced to take on commissions in order to keep the lights on at Zoetrope - like *Peggy Sue Got Married* (1986). After production was finished, tragedy struck the Coppola family - 22-year-old Gio died in a boating accident. Meanwhile, *Gardens of Stone* (1987) and *Tucker: The Man and his Dream* were highly personal, albeit unsuccessful, projects for Coppola, ending the decade on a low note.

In 1990, Coppola agreed to direct a third installment of *The Godfather* series, which he firmly describes as an epilogue rather than an official part of a trilogy. Fans of the previous films came back in droves to watch the conclusion of Michael Corleone's meteoric rise and fall. Despite mixed reviews (and scathing criticism of Sofia Coppola's performance as Mary Corleone), the film made nearly $140 million worldwide. After that, Coppola made *Bram Stoker's Dracula* (1992), also a success, *Jack* (1996), starring Robin Williams, and *The Rainmaker* (1997), based on the bestselling novel by John Grisham. Bankable once more, Coppola re-cut and re-released *Apocalypse Now* as *Apocalypse Now Redux.* After a 10-year hiatus, he produced and directed three films, *Youth without Youth* (2007), *Tetro* (2009) and *Twixt* (2011) - small, intimate pieces that did not have much of an impact financially or critically.

Despite periods of fluctuating success, Francis Ford Coppola remains an icon of cinema, though he has mostly passed the cinematic torch to a younger generation. His daughter, Sofia, and nephew, Nicolas Cage, have gone on to Oscar-winning careers, and his son, Roman, is a successful screenwriter and director. Francis Ford Coppola still runs Zoetrope Virtual Studio for filmmakers, as well as Cafe Zoetrope, inside the Sentinel Building where American Zoetrope has its offices. He also owns the Inglebrook Winery and lifestyle brand *Francis Ford Coppola Presents.* In 1997, he started a literary magazine called *Zoetrope: All-Story*, for which he is still the founding editor and publisher.

About Apocalypse Now

Apocalypse Now, Francis Ford Coppola's 1979 tour de force epic about the Vietnam War, is a rare film where the infamously perilous shoot rivaled the onscreen drama. At his Cannes press conference, after unveiling the (yet unfinished) cut, Coppola himself said, "We had access to too much money, too much equipment. We built villages in the jungle and the weather destroyed them, and we went insane. Eventually I realized that I was not making the movie. The movie was making itself - or the jungle was making it for me" (Cowie 131).

Ten years earlier, in 1969, John Milius wrote the screenplay for *Apocalypse Now*. While at UCLA, Milius' mentor, Francis Ford Coppola, claimed that *Heart of Darkness* was impossible to adapt - even the great Orson Welles had failed to crack it. Milius decided that he was up to the challenge, updating the setting from the French-occupied Congo to the Vietnam War - a subject, according to Peter Biskind, that "was still too sensitive for Hollywood to touch" (Biskind 246). According to Milius, the title is based on "a button badge popular among hippies during the 1960s - [that read] 'Nirvana Now'" (Cowie 120).

Originally, George Lucas was the intended director, planning to make *Apocalypse Now* as a $2 million documentary-style film about Vietnam with real soldiers. Lucas had done some prep work already, but he knew "no studio would finance a film on the Vietnam War while it was still raging" (Cowie 5). He thought that making *American Graffiti* first would give him the status and clout he would need to get *Apocalypse Now* off the ground. After that film was done, though, Lucas got swept up in an epic of his own: *Star Wars*.

However, by 1974, Francis Ford Coppola was fresh off the massive success of *The Godfather* films and recognized the timeliness of *Apocalypse Now*. With Lucas otherwise engaged, Coppola decided to direct the film himself. He figured it would make a lot of money and finally resuscitate his studio Zoetrope's financial stability. "My thought was to do some virtuoso directing, and get on with what I'd always thought I wanted to do - which is which is to have my own film company, and my own studio, and really get to work" (Cowie 7). Coppola thought that *Apocalypse Now* would be his opportunity to make a film easily. Walter Murch says that Coppola imagined it as "a big outdoor opera...he thought he would be in his shorts, run around in the jungle, swim, and make a film that was far from the kinds of issues and dynamics that he had previously worked on" (Cowie 7). He could not have been more wrong.

Apocalypse Now was the most difficult film of Coppola's career, more challenging than most directors will experience in a lifetime. "It was a hellish shoot, the difficulties compounded by Coppola's arrogance" (Biskind 347). The US Department of Defense would not support the film and rejected producer Fred Roos' requests for military advisors, escorts, aircrafts, vehicles, and radios. However, the Filipino government, specifically, President Ferdinand Marcos, was much more amenable - making it the most attractive location for the shoot, despite the risk of political upheaval and unpredictable weather.

In October 1975, The Philippines Department of National Defense signed a contract with Coppola, agreeing to provide the production with equipment, personnel, and "twenty Huey helicopters for the aerial attack sequence" (Cowie 16). On paper, it seemed perfect - but in practice, the situation was not so simple. The Filipino government kept pulling the helicopters off set to fight the rebel forces that were rising up in the southern part of the country, leading to extensive delays.

That wasn't the only challenge, though. After a month of shooting in the Philippines with Harvey Keitel in the role of Willard, Coppola fired him and re-cast the role with Martin Sheen, which necessitated re-shoots for all of Keitel's scenes and put the film even further behind schedule. Coppola was constantly rewriting the screenplay on set, a practice that had worked for him before, but the stakes were much higher this time. As a result, the crew never knew what scenes were being shot when they arrived on set, and would not have a chance to prepare adequately. In addition, the heat was vicious and the hours were long, and after hours the cast and crew would party as hard as they worked - Coppola included. He is rumored to have thrown himself an $8,000 party for his 37th birthday.

In addition, Coppola's nasty temper emerged regularly - he was throwing things at his crew, firing people, and trashing equipment. Certainly, his recent success had affected his ego, but he became increasingly concerned that *Apocalypse Now* was going to be a massive, career-ending failure. In the midst of the shoot, Coppola's wife, Eleanor, wrote in her diary: "More and more, it seems like there are parallels between the character of Kurtz and Francis. There is the exhilaration of power in the face of losing everything, like the excitement of war when one kills and takes the chances of being killed" (Cowie 123).

When it looked like things couldn't get any worse, on May 19, 1976, Typhoon Didang (or Olga) hit the Philippines. It was the worst storm the region had seen in 40 years. The storm destroyed many of *Apocalypse Now*'s sets. The crew was stranded, some of them without electricity or drinking water (Coppola, meanwhile, was shacked up in a hotel with a porn actress). The production had to be shut down. Coppola returned to San Francisco "with ninety hours of rushes and only 8 minutes of cut, usable film" (Biskind 351). By this point, the production was 6 weeks behind schedule, and nearly $3 million over budget. Coppola did not yet have a completed script and the end was nowhere in sight. The director was forced to make a difficult deal with United Artists for a $3 million loan - if *Apocalypse Now* did not earn over $40,000,000, Coppola himself would be personally responsible for paying the studio back.

So began the second phase of production on *Apocalypse Now*, and Coppola returned to the Philippines to pick up where he left off. Soon, the lavish set for the Kurtz compound had been rebuilt. Marlon Brando, who was to be paid $1 million a week to play the role of Kurtz, brought with him a whole new set of challenges: he wanted to sleep on a houseboat, he was terrifically overweight and insecure about it, and he had done no preparation for his part as Kurtz - he had not even read *Heart of Darkness*. Coppola was still struggling to figure out a way to end the film. Despite his limited shoot days, Brando wanted to spend hours discussing his character with Coppola, holding up the shoot endlessly. As the days dragged on, Coppola was losing control and his behavior was getting increasingly erratic, much to his wife's concern. She wrote in her diary, "It is scary to watch someone you love go into the center of himself and confront his fears, fear of failure, fear of death, fear of going insane" (Cowie 126). Between Francis' flagrant infidelity and rampant self-doubt, the Coppolas' marriage was in trouble.

On March 5, 1977, Martin Sheen had a heart attack. Needless to say, the anxiety on set was palpable, and it spread all the way back to the United Artists offices in New York City. Coppola was furious with his assistant for letting the news of Sheen's ill health reach all the way to the States, and UA's concerns made him even more determined to keep shooting. They shot whatever they could without their star and when Sheen recovered a month later, went back and finished shooting all his close-ups. Finally on May 21, 1977, 14 months after the first day of shooting and 238 days of production, *Apocalypse Now* wrapped. Coppola's struggle was not over yet, though - post production lay ahead.

Peter Cowie writes, "for almost two years, [the post-production team] would toil in Rutherford, San Francisco, and Los Angeles to draw structure from the raw marble of the movie brought back from the Philippines" (Cowie 99). One major component of the editing process was to craft the narration - for which Coppola brought in Michael Herr. Famed sound editor Walter Murch had very little to work with by way of live sound - the tight schedule had prevented the production sound team from getting clean dialogue and effects. Back then, effects libraries did not have contemporary war sounds, and so Murch and his colleagues crafted the jungle soundscape from scratch. Ultimately, Murch would be rewarded with an Academy Award for his innovative techniques.

Much to Francis Ford Coppola's (and United Artists') relief and joy, *Apocalypse Now* was a hit, grossing $75 million during its United States theatrical run. It won the Palme d'Or at the 1979 Cannes Film Festival (Coppola's second after *The Conversation*). Even though a few critics were divided on the film - *Time* Magazine's Frank Rich called it "emotionally obtuse and intellectually empty," It was nominated for 8 Academy Awards - Besides Murch, cinematographer Vittorio Storaro also took home an Oscar for his work. Today, The American Film Institute ranks *Apocalypse Now* #19 on the list of greatest films of the 20th Century. Coppola's embattled masterpiece has lived on in both pop culture and as major triumph of American filmmaking, capturing a moment in history right as it was occurring. As Coppola said in a press conference - "the film is not about Vietnam. It *is* Vietnam".

Character List

Willard

Captain Benjamin L. Willard is played by Martin Sheen. He is formerly 505 Battalion, 173rd Airborne, assigned to MACV-SOG (Military Assistance Command, Vietnam - Studies and Observations Group). He has undertaken a number of special operations for the U.S. Army and the CIA and is well versed in COMSEC. His final mission is to track down and kill renegade Col. Walter E. Kurtz.

Willard completed one tour of Vietnam and then returned home to the United States, where he was unable to re-adapt to his normal life. He and his wife divorced, and Willard returned to Saigon. He is clearly unsettled at the beginning of the film, completely drunk and high in a Saigon hotel room. Over the course of the film, Willard is only able to address the darkness in his own heart as he gets closer and closer to Kurtz. His character is loosely based on Charles Marlow in Joseph Conrad's *Heart of Darkness*.

Lt. General Corman

Lieutenant General Corman, Military Intelligence (G-2) is played by G.D. Spradlin. He is from the American south, and exhibits good manners, even though he is responsible for assigning Willard to his classified mission to track down and kill Kurtz.

Col. Lucas

Colonel Lucas, played by Harrison Ford, is the other military officer, along with Lt. General Corman, who assigns Willard his mission.

Kilgore

Lieutenant Colonel Bill Kilgore, played by Robert Duvall, is the Commanding Officer of 1st Squadron, 9th Air Cavalry Regiment. He is confident and filled with bravado. He has an air of absurdity, leading him to do things like send his soldiers out to surf in the middle of a battle and play *Ride of the Valkyries* during an airborne attack. He is a surfing fanatic, and gets very excited when he finds out that Lance Johnson is on Willard's PBR.

Chef

3rd Class Jay "Chef" Hicks, played by Frederic Forrest, is part of Willard's crew. He is a machinist from New Orleans, whom Willard describes as "wrapped too tight." Out of Willard's crew, he is the most affected by the brutality of the war. He has an affinity for smoking marijuana and looks forward to letters from his girlfriend, Eva. Before the war, Chef was studying to become a saucier. He dies by decapitation at Kurtz's compound.

Lance

Lance B. Johnson, played by Sam Bottoms, is a famous surfer from Los Angeles who is now Gunner's Mate, 3rd Class L. He is tan and blonde and has a handsome baby face. He enjoys psychedelic drugs, especially acid. Over the course of the film, he appears to become more and more spacey, speaking infrequently and painting his face. While at Kurtz's compound, Lance is enchanted by the Montagnard tribe, even participating in their final sacrifice ritual. Eventually, Willard pulls Lance back onto the PBR - the two men are the sole survivors of the mission.

Mr. Clean

Tyrone "Clean" Miller, played by Laurence Fishburne (who was only 14 at the time), is 17 years old when he joins Willard's mission. He is from the South Bronx. Clean and Chief develop a father-son bond. He displays arrogant behavior, drumming on the boat and playing loud rock music, which annoys Willard. He also opens fire on a sampan full of innocent Vietnamese people. Clean dies after being hit by Viet Cong fire from inside the jungle.

Chief

Chief Quartermaster George Phillips, played by Albert Hall, is the commander of the PBR that takes Willard and his crew up the Nung River. He is serious and usually tries to follow the rules, leading to frequent clashes with Willard. He eventually dies after being stabbed through the heart by a spear after the PBR ventures into Cambodia.

Photojournalist

A manic American journalist and follower of Kurtz, played by (the equally unstable) Dennis Hopper. He greets the PBR as it arrives at Kurtz's compound for the first time. The character of the Photojournalist is based on Sean Flynn (the son of actor Errol Flynn), a news correspondent who disappeared in Cambodia in 1970, and the Russian "harlequin" from *Heart of Darkness.*

Kurtz

Col. Walter E. Kurtz, played by Marlon Brando, was a highly decorated member of the U.S. Army Special Forces and the 5th Special Forces Group. However, he has gone rogue and is running his own command out of Cambodia. He is a powerful man, feared by the American military as well as the Viet Cong, the Cambodians, and the NVA. He has a wife and a son back home, whom he still cares about, but he is too far gone to ever return to his pre-war life. Kurtz is based on the character of Kurtz from *Heart of Darkness.*

Captain Richard M. Colby

Played by Scott Glenn, Colby was assigned to kill Kurtz, but instead, he defected and joined Kurtz's army. Originally, he was thought to be dead, but Willard receives a memo at Do Lung bridge containing Colby's missive to his wife, instructing her to sell all their possessions (and their children) because he is never coming back. Willard recognizes Colby at Kurtz's compound, but he never speaks.

The Promoter

Or the "agent," played by Bill Graham, is in charge of the USO Show where 3 *Playboy* Playmates perform for the troops at Hau Phat. After the troops become rowdy and start pawing at the playmates, The Promoter must hustle the girls back into the helicopter and take them to safety.

Civilian

The third man, (played by Jerry Ziesmer) present at Willard's initial briefing, who only speaks one line: "Terminate. With Extreme Prejudice."

Playboy Bunnies

Cynthia Wood (1971 Playmate of the Year), Linda (Beatty) Carpenter (August 1976 Playmate), and Colleen Camp ("Miss May" Playmate).

Major Themes

Detachment

Midway through the Vietnam War, many American soldiers felt a level of detachment stemming from a general lack of understanding as to why they were there. Others performed unadulterated acts of violence simply because they thought they were fulfilling a duty. Either way, the patriotic "war hero" figure that emerged after World War II was fully shattered for many young soldiers, and Coppola expresses this in several instances in *Apocalypse Now*. Kilgore has made a sport out of killing, eviscerating an entire village in order to move the PBR to the mouth of the Nung River. He celebrates the drama of killing by playing *Ride of the Valkyries* on a loudspeaker to signal the arrival of his Air Cavalry. On a smaller scale, Mr. Clean opens fire on a sampan of innocent Vietnamese people before Chef is able to discern if they are dangerous or not. Throughout, the soldiers who perpetrate feats of grotesque violence do not seem to process the full weight of their actions.

Desperation

There are many levels of desperation in *Apocalypse Now*. From the opening scene, it is evident that Willard is fighting his inner demons, and has returned to Saigon because he does not recognize his pre-Vietnam life anymore. The sailors on the PBR are desperate to finish their duty and return home alive, especially Chef. This is clearly a common feeling amongst the American troops - soldiers cling to the landing skids of the Playboy Bunnies' helicopter, and when the PBR pulls into the murky scene around the Do Lung Bridge, soldiers actually jump into the water for a chance at a ride home. These characters are in contrast with those who are in Vietnam with an expressed mission: Willard, Kurtz, and Kilgore. The atmosphere of desperation helps Coppola's achieve his desire to depict the Vietnam War as it was for the people on the ground.

Exploitation

Exploitation existed on both sides of the conflict in Vietnam - on the war front and at home. Both Kurtz and Willard speak about the lies surrounding the American presence there. Kurtz is, in effect, a representation of the ugly truth: millions of innocents, both Americans and Vietnamese, are dying as a result of the American political agenda. We see this in Kilgore's air raid, in which the Air Cavalry takes out an entire village for the purpose of moving the PBR upriver. Meanwhile, Willard comments that the American tactic is to "cut [The Vietnamese] in half with machine gun and give them a band-aid." A big part of the Vietnam War narrative is the way that the American media kept trying to sell it to the public, praising the war effort day after day. Ultimately, the war was political maneuvering, plain and simple, and has created a stain on American history.

Journey

Like Joseph Conrad's novel on which the film is loosely based, Coppola structures the narrative of *Apocalypse Now* as a journey. Willard arrives in Saigon with the goal of being assigned to a new mission, because after his first tour of Vietnam, he no longer fits into his civilian life. Therefore, his journey to find Kurtz is both literal and metaphorical - a journey into the jungle and into himself. On the way, he was forced to address the darkest corners of his soul. The only way Willard can reject Kurtz is to see himself in Kurtz. Kurtz, meanwhile, knows his time has come but gives Willard a new mission: to go back to America and tell Kurtz's son the truth about his father. In this way, Willard's first mission is to uncover the dirty truths behind the Vietnam War, and his future journey is to reveal them to the people at home.

Throughout the production, Francis Ford Coppola was not unlike his protagonist. The director's wife, Eleanor, wrote in her journal that she saw her husband going through his own transformative experience during production. Like Willard, Coppola was taking his crew deep into the heart of the jungle, and had to face enormous difficulties and emotional issues in order to tell the story he wanted to tell while keeping his life - and his sanity - in tact.

Accountability

One of the lingering controversies surrounding the Vietnam War is that of accountability. In one particularly brutal example, the My Lai Massacre (where 100 American Soldiers massacred over 500 innocent Vietnamese civilians over the course of 4 hours), resulted in very little judiciary action. *Apocalypse Now*, however, examines the impact of personal accountability. Although every soldier in the film has to commit some level of atrocity in the name of patriotism, these brutal acts eat away at a man's humanity. Kurtz, meanwhile, has seen such horrors that he can no longer climb out of his own darkness, but after their encounter, Willard learns to accept that darkness inside himself and chooses to suppress it. As he walks out of the temple after killing Kurtz, he could easily step into Kurtz's position, but he chooses not to. He holds himself accountable, even if his followers would not.

Innocence

The most controversial aspect of the Vietnam War was the number of innocent people who suffered on both sides. Coppola depicts shattered innocence in a number of ways throughout *Apocalypse Now*. When Willard boards the PBR, he describes his crew as "rock and rollers with one foot in their graves," implying that they are fun-loving young people naive to the brutality that lies ahead. During the sampan massacre, Coppola makes this point with heavy symbolism - Mr. Clean shoots everyone on the boat after a woman tries too hard to protect the contents of a woven basket. After the other passengers are dead, Chef discovers that there is a puppy in the basket, which Lance adopts and keeps close to him. After young Mr. Clean is killed, the puppy disappears. In the film, Lance remains a figure of childlike innocence. He keeps the puppy close to his chest to protect it from gunfire. He gives Chief a respectful burial at sea. When they arrive at Kurtz's compound, he shoots down a corpse hanging from a tree. He holds onto whatever shreds of humanity he can find in the dark, menacing jungle.

Insanity

The question of insanity underlies the driving force of Willard's entire mission against Kurtz. When Corman briefs Willard, he offers his own practical explanation of Kurtz's crimes: "Every man has got a breaking point. You and I have. Walter Kurtz has reached his. And very obviously, he has gone insane." While Corman alleges that Kurtz's paranoia led to him murdering four South Vietnamese intelligence agents, Kurtz writes in his letters home that it's the charges against him that are insane. While Kurtz has snapped, he is very lucid about many of his decisions - and that is terrifying to the men who are supposed to be controlling him. On the other side, Kilgore is similarly over the top. He actually likes to have a soundtrack to his air raids, and makes his soldiers go surfing in the middle of gunfire. Yet, Kilgore is on one side of the war, a hero, and Kurtz is on the other, a menace. Kurtz, meanwhile, defines whatever has happened to him as the ultimate clarity, and he sees men like Willard as lacking agency: "errand boy[s] sent by grocery clerks to collect the bill." Insanity on the battlefield is a common trope used in works of art depicting life during wartime (*The Red Badge of Courage*, *Catch-22*, *Slaughterhouse Five*, etc.), but Coppola's exploration of blurred morality is appropriately visceral as the Vietnam War itself was muddied in purpose.

Glossary of Terms

AFVN

Armed Forces Vietnam Network is a radio station that provided US soldiers with radio and television programs during the Vietnam war. It kept the troops informed and entertained.

Airborne

Refers to military units set up to be moved by aircraft and "dropped" into battle. They can be placed easily behind enemy lines and deploy in unexpected places with very little warning.

C.O.

Short for "Commanding Officer" - an officer in command of a military unit.

Charles Manson

A convicted felon who became notorious for his leadership of the Manson family, a quasi-cult in California in the 1960s. The Manson family carried out several murders that rocked Hollywood - their victims included the pregnant actress Sharon Tate and Leno and Rosemary LaBianca.

Charlie

Slang for Viet Cong. The term is short for the phonetic spelling (used by the military and police to spell things over the radio) of "VC," which is "Victor Charlie."

ComSec

Short for Communications Security.

Death Cards

The American soldiers' practice of leaving individual Ace of Spades playing cards on Vietnamese corpses as a psychological weapon against VC soldiers.

Dialectics

Inquiry into metaphysical contradictions and their solutions.

Dink

A disparaging term for a North Vietnamese soldier or guerrilla fighter.

Dossier

A collection of documents about a particular person, event, or subject.

Double Agent

An agent who pretends to act as a spy for one country or organization while in fact acting on behalf of an enemy.

Green Beret

Highly skilled special forces in the US Army.

Hairy

Slang for "dangerous".

Hueys

Nickname for the Bell UH-1 Iroquois, a Vietnam-era multipurpose helicopter.

Montagnards

The indigenous people of the Central Highlands of Vietnam.

Napalm

A substance made from petrol that was used in bombs by US forces to burn fields and villages during the Vietnam War. Images of Vietnamese victims suffering from napalm burns helped make people question U.S. tactics and the war in general.

Pagan

A person holding religious beliefs other than those of the main world religions.

PBR

Short for Patrol Boat, River. A boat used in the Vietnam War to travel shallow waters. Each PBR typically held a crew of 4 men and was armed with guns and grenade launchers.

R&R

Military slang for "Rest and Relaxation" or "Rest and Recuperation". In Vietnam, soldiers qualified for one week of R&R to an approved destination. After serving for six months, a soldier could put his name on a list to be selected for a vacation to Bangkok, Hong Kong, Japan, Australia, Hawaii, Taiwan, or Singapore.

Sampan

A Sampan is a 3.5 - 4.5 meter long flat-bottomed boat. It is of Chinese origin, and is used by many traditional and rural South-East Asian populations as a fishing and transport vessel. Sampans were used extensively by Vietnamese people during wartime.

The Doors

An American rock band led by charismatic lead singer Jim Morrison. They were extremely popular and controversial during the late 60s and early 70s because of Morrison's wild behavior and poetic lyrics. He eventually died from an overdose in 1971.

USO

The United Service Organizations Inc. (USO Show) is a nonprofit organization that provides programs, services and live entertainment to United States troops and their families.

Short Summary

Under The Doors' "This is the End," a helicopter bombs a strip of jungle, which ignites in flames. Dissolve to Captain Benjamin L. Willard, who is drunk and high in a Saigon hotel room. In his voice-over, he says that this is his second tour of duty in Vietnam, and he is waiting for his next assignment. Two soldiers arrive in his hotel room and throw him in the shower to sober him up. Willard is brought to ComSec Intelligence in Nha Trang to be debriefed.

Willard arrives in Nha Trang via helicopter and meets Lt. General Corman and Col. Lucas for lunch. They supply him with information about Col Walter E. Kurtz, who was a celebrated Operations Officer with the 5th Special Forces until he broke away from his assignment and has, by all counts, gone insane. He is currently in Cambodia, having amassed a large local following. Additionally, he ordered the assassination of some South Vietnamese intelligence agents that he was convinced were spies and is now wanted for murder. Willard's mission is to travel up the Nung River and terminate Kurtz's command "with extreme prejudice."

Willard's transport to the Nung River is a Navy patrol boat (AKA a Patrol Boat, River, or PBR). His crew consists of The Chef, Lance, Mr. Clean, and Phillips "The Chief," who captains the boat. They start on their journey, seemingly carefree. While the crew listens to the radio and soaks in the sun, Willard sits quietly in the back of the boat and studies Kurtz's dossier, trying to understand the man's motivations. Soon, the boat crosses paths with the Air Cavalry Division - 1st of the 9th, led by Captain Kilgore. Kilgore is tasked with taking Willard and the PBR to the mouth of the Nung River. The Air Cav is in full-on attack mode, destroying a Vietnamese Village. At first, Kilgore is dismissive but then becomes energized when he hears that Lance Johnson, the famous surfer, is among Willard's crew.

That night, Kilgore hosts a beach party and promises to get the PBR to the mouth of the Nung River, despite the fact that they will have to pass through a Viet Cong stronghold. The next day, the Air Cav airlifts the PBR to its next destination, while Willard and his crew ride along in helicopters. Kilgore likes to play "Ride of the Valkyries" while conducting airstrikes. Kilgore's team successfully destroys the village after calling in a napalm strike, allowing Willard and his crew to continue on their journey.

Back on the boat, Chef gets very stoned and decides to go out into the jungle in search of mangoes. Willard accompanies him, but instead of fruit, they are chased by a tiger. Chef howls madly, "never get out of the boat!" Willard considers Kurtz, who got off the boat and "split from the whole fucking program." He continues reading Kurtz's dossier, and learns that Kurtz had a history of carrying out missions without official clearance, but in the past he had been praised as a hero because Operation Arcangel was a major success. The PBR arrives at Hau Phat where there is a supply warehouse and an upcoming USO show. Willard and his crew are in the bleachers while three American Playboy Playmates dance provocatively for the troops. However, their show is cut short when the over-excited soldiers storm the stage and start pawing at the dancing women. The Playmates are herded into their helicopter and shuttled back home.

The next morning, the PBR moves on up the river towards the Do Lung Bridge. Along the way, Willard continues to pore over Kurtz's dossier. He sees photographs of Kurtz's camp in Cambodia. Everyone - Charlie included - is afraid of Kurtz. Willard comments that the Army has "lost him." Meanwhile, Chief is becoming more concerned about their mystery destination. Willard tells him where they are going - Cambodia. He promises that if Chief can take him as close to the destination as possible, he will let the PBR go back and continue on alone. Later, Willard reads a letter that Kurtz wrote to his son, claiming that the charges against him are insane and accuses the American Army of having "timid morality."

The PBR crosses paths with a Vietnamese sampan, crewed by civilians. According to protocol, Chief makes Chef raid the Sampan to make sure that the sailors are not trafficking supplies to the Viet Cong. A woman onboard won't let him go through her basket, and so Mr. Clean suddenly opens fire and massacres everyone on the sampan. It turns out that the woman, who is still (barely) alive, was only trying to save a puppy, which Lance keeps. Chief wants to take the woman to get help but Willard kills her and tells the crew that they are moving on.

They arrive at the Do Lung Bridge, the last army outpost on the Nung River, at nightfall. Lt. Carson has been waiting for the PBR and delivers an official Army memo to Willard and a bag of mail for the rest of the crew. The outpost is in a state of chaos - every night, Charlie finds a way to blow up the bridge and every day, the Americans rebuild it. Lance, who is tripping on acid, accompanies Willard to shore in an attempt to find the commanding officer - but there is none. They return to the PBR and continue up the river, despite Chief's hesitation.

Willard reads the memo from the Army, which says that Capt. Richard Colby, the last man sent on a mission to find Kurtz, actually defected and has joined Kurtz's followers. Mr. Clean listens to a taped message from his mother when suddenly a cascade of bullets bursts out from the jungle. The crew immediately returns fire, but it's too late - Clean dies with his mother's voice still playing on the tape. Chief bawls over Clean's body. Later, Chef becomes wild with paranoia and Willard claims that Kurtz is close - he can feel his presence. The PBR is attacked again by Kurtz's followers. Willard tries to get his crew not to retaliate, since the arrows are harmless, but they don't listen. A spear pierces Chief through the heart. Before he dies, he uses all his strength to grip Willard's throat, furious as to what he's led them into. Later, Chef and Lance agree to accompany Willard all the way to his final destination.

Finally, the PBR arrives at Kurtz's compound. They are greeted by the Photojournalist, an American civilian who has been documenting Kurtz and his activities. Willard and Lance go on land and see Capt. Colby, who refuses to speak.

The steps to the temple where Kurtz lives are covered in human heads. The Photojournalist insists that Kurtz is a great man but that he sometimes just goes too far. Back on the PBR, Chef is scared, calling Kurtz evil and saying he'll do anything to kill the man and get out of there. Willard decides to take Lance with him back to land to find Kurtz, and tells Chef to radio in an airstrike if they are not back by 2200 hours.

On land, Kurtz's followers descend upon Willard and bring him to Kurtz. Kurtz, from the shadows, calls Willard an "errand boy sent by grocery clerks to collect the bill." Later, Willard, showing signs of torture, is imprisoned in a bamboo cage. The Photojournalist tries to convince him that Kurtz is a genius. On the PBR, Chef realizes that it's time to call in the airstrike. At night, Willard is hunched in his cage when Kurtz comes out, standing right by him, face painted in camouflage. He drops Chef's severed head onto Willard's lap.

In the morning, two men carry Willard into Kurtz's quarters, where he stays for days, voluntarily. He claims not to know what he will do and wonders how Kurtz's family and former colleagues would react if they knew how far gone he was. Kurtz tells Willard that he has the right to kill him but not to judge him - they have both witnessed the same horrors in this war. He asks Willard to tell his son the truth about him. Later, when it's dark, Kurtz's followers conduct a ritual sacrifice of a water buffalo while Willard kills Kurtz with a knife. Afterwards, Willard emerges onto the steps of the temple and the crowd kneels before him. Willard, however, drops his knife, takes Lance by the hand, and steers the PBR back down the river. He turns off the radio, buzzing with voices from Trang, and hears Kurtz's last whispered words echoing in his mind: "The horror...the horror."

Quotes and Analysis

"It was no accident that I got to be the caretaker of Colonel Walter E. Kurtz's memory, any more than being back in Saigon was an accident. There is no way to tell his story without telling my own. And if his story is really a confession, then so is mine"

Capt. Willard, 00:09:47

This statement and the fact that most of the voiceover is in the past tense indicates that the events of *Apocalypse Now* are illustrative of Willard's recollections. This sets the tone for the film, because Coppola gives his audience the expectation of a transformative journey, but also, we know that Willard is going to survive and Kurtz is going to die. By calling himself the 'caretaker of Kurtz's memory,' Willard foreshadows the decision he makes at the end of the film. When Willard first arrives at Kurtz's compound, it seems as though Kurtz only keeps Willard alive because he wants to give him all the knowledge and guilt so he can take Kurtz's place. Once Kurtz has accepted that his time has come, he entrusts Willard with a mission that will take him back out of the jungle. Kurtz wants Willard to share his story, all of it, with his own son. Therefore, even though Kurtz deserves to perish for all his moral violations, Willard understands why he snapped, and can hopefully, use Kurtz's story to prevent another Vietnam.

"There's a conflict in every human heart between the rational and the irrational, between good and evil. And good does not always triumph. Sometimes, a dark side overcomes what Lincoln called, 'the better angels of our nature.' Every man has got a breaking point. You and I have them. Walter Kurtz has reached his, and very obviously, he has gone insane."

General Corman, 00:15:57

The irony in this statement is that although General Corman is explaining to Willard what has happened to Kurtz, he cannot see the same darkness that he has a hand in perpetrating. Kurtz has reached his breaking point, certainly, but he knows it. He is entirely aware that the Americans are out to get him, but he does not respect his own country's army enough to follow their rules anymore. General Corman is a symbol of many military leaders in Vietnam who held onto the traditional values of war and cavalry. He does not question his own purpose in Vietnam, but can isolate Kurtz in a box of "insanity," without understanding how he got there. Like Kilgore, it is not Corman's job to question. It is his goal to explain the reason for the problem and "terminate" it.

"Do you smell that? Do you smell that? Napalm, son. Nothing else in the world smells like that. I love the smell of napalm in the morning. You know, one time we

had a hail bomb for 12 hours and when it was all over, I walked up. We didn't find one of them, not one stinking Dink body. But the smell, like that gasoline smell. The whole hill. Smelled like...victory. Someday this war's gonna end."

Capt. Kilgore, 00:49:16

Kilgore is an over-the-top character, completely absurd and in line with Coppola's dark sense of humor. Napalm is not a smell to be loved - in 1980, the United Nations declared that the use of it on concentrations of civilians constituted a war crime. Kilgore, though, as Willard describes, thinks of himself as invincible. He does not get bogged down with ideological questioning, but rather, he knows how to make the act of war satisfying for himself. Even if that means bombing an entire village for the purpose of catching a 6-foot wave, he will do it. He does, however, display loyalty to his own men, hurrying injured troops to the hospital. Peter Cowie cites John Milius, who once said, "war is unspeakably attractive. People enjoy intensity. The human animal seems drawn to it like a moth to a flame". When the war ends, Kilgore won't be lamenting the lives he's taken. He will be a hero in his own mind, and live on to fight - and revel in - the next one.

"Someday, this war's gonna end. That'd be just fine with the boys on the boat. They weren't looking for anything more than a way home. Trouble is, I'd been back there and I knew that it just didn't exist anymore."

Willard, 00:50:30

This quote captures the divide between Willard and the crew on the PBR. Many of the young men who went to Vietnam, like the PBR crew, did not really understand why they were there. Vietnam ended up being the most unpopular war in American history, and many soldiers were just desperate to finish their tours and get home. They did not realize how the war would live with them; the psychological repercussions of brutality lingered at home. Willard is on his second tour voluntarily. He went home and was haunted by the things he had seen and done in Vietnam. Therefore, his journey up the Nung River is a mission to kill Kurtz, but it is also a way for him to address his own demons - this is the only way for him to ever learn to live with himself. The other crew members, though, just want to complete the mission and get home, not knowing that (if they survive), they will be as hardened and damaged as Willard.

"They lost him. He was gone. Nothing but rumors and random intelligence, mostly from captured V.C. The V.C. knew his name by now, and they were scared of him. He and his men were playing hit-and-run all the way into Cambodia."

Willard, 01:10:21

Kurtz is terrifying to the American military because they no longer have control over him. Kilgore, on the other hand, harbors dangerous delusions of grandeur, but he is firmly on the American side. Were Kurtz employing his "unsound methods" on Charlie within the confines of Vietnam, he'd likely be a hero. Kurtz beheading his Montagnard followers in fits of madness is not so far off from Kilgore napalming a village so that one PBR can pass through. Kurtz, however, is playing by his own rules, which is terrifying to both sides. He seems to have some kind of power that neither the USA or the VC seem to understand, and instead of trying to figure him out, they'd rather eliminate him. With extreme prejudice.

"It was a way we had over here of living with ourselves. We'd cut 'em in half with a machine gun and give 'em a band-aid. It was a lie. And the more I saw of them, the more I hated lies."

Willard, 01:21:07

At this point in the journey, Willard is dealing with his guilt of "participating in the excesses of war" (Cowie 142). He understands that the atrocities the Americans are committing in Vietnam highly outweigh the benefits. This quote invokes the dichotomy that many Vietnam vets, like Willard, experienced during their service (and a common sentiment in veterans of the Iraq War many decades later) - that while they are supposedly fighting for a noble cause, their actions on the ground feel more like unbridled brutality. Coppola's aim in making *Apocalypse Now* was to show Vietnam as it was for the men who fought there - the mysterious, elusive enemy, the lack of leadership, the confusion, the alienation, the guilt - far beyond what the media portrayed. The fictional camera crew in the film is only interested in capturing images of soldiers in battle as heroes even though that is only a tiny part of the real situation.

I used to think that if I died in an evil place, than my soul wouldn't be able to make it to heaven. But now, fuck. I mean, I don't care where it goes as long as it ain't here."

The Chef, 01:51:48

The main dichotomy at the core of *Apocalypse Now* is the fight between good and evil that, like General Corman says when giving Willard his mission, exists inside every man. Chef is especially sensitive to the horrors he has witnessed during his duty. He has a number of outbursts throughout the film, and in this quote, he seems to have accepted his fate. He knows he is not an innocent anymore, but the darkness that Kurtz represents is simply too much for him to bear. Unlike Willard, Chef has no desire to hear what Kurtz has to say or understand why the Colonel has snapped. He is ready to decimate the place and try to forget it forever, which is why Kurtz cannot let him survive. Kurtz knows his time has come to an end, but he needs to pass on his guilt and anoint a messenger - Willard.

"Are you an assassin?"

"I'm a soldier."

"You're neither. You're an errand boy. Sent by grocery clerks. To collect the bill"

Kurtz and Willard, 01:58:20

By this point in the film, Coppola has made it clear that there is no real divide between an assassin and a soldier, in his point of view. Kurtz draws Willard's (and the audience's) attention to the lack of agency that Willard and his fellow soldiers have in determining their actions. Ultimately, Willard has been both a soldier and an assassin, but Kurtz is drawing attention to the fact that the separation is in name alone. Willard has come to assassinate Kurtz as part of his duty as a soldier, because he is beholden to the army. Without the umbrella of an official mission, men like Willard and Kilgore are simply assassins. Meanwhile, just because Kurtz is operating outside of the Army's jurisdiction, he has crossed the line from soldier to assassin, although the Army is committing much greater atrocities than Kurtz is.

"If the generals back in the Trang could see what I saw. Would they still want me to kill him? More than ever, probably. Then what would his people back home want if they ever learned just how far from them he'd really gone? He broke from them, and then he broke from himself. I'd never seen a man so broken up and ripped apart."

Willard, 02:08:54

When Willard first encounters Kurtz, he is intimidated by him - a man who was once on such an elite track, has now gone completely awry. In this quote, Willard (reflecting back on this experience, since his voiceover is all in the past tense) explains the ideological core of his journey into the jungle. Kurtz is a liability to "his people back home," which is why Gen. Corman and his superiors want him dead. However, Kurtz did not just wake up one day and decide to go rogue - he unraveled over time, as Willard discovers as he examines Kurtz's dossier. As a result of his participation in this war, Kurtz lost trust in the leaders he had been loyal to his whole life and ended up questioning the whole essence of his being. Therein lies the hypocrisy of the American presence in Vietnam; instead of trying to understand and alleviate the circumstances that would drive such a great man to such extreme lengths, they would rather conceal his existence with even more lies.

"You have to have men who are moral and at the same time who are able to utilize their primordial instincts to kill, without feeling, without passion, without judgement."

Kurtz, 02:13:21

Kurtz describes witnessing the VC chop off the arms of a group of Vietnamese children whom the Americans had recently inoculated. In this particular quote, Kurtz professes his admiration of his opponents and their ability to turn off the disgust and programmed morality that Kurtz himself has succumbed to. In a broader sense, Coppola is pointing out that the American military lacked any unity or purpose. These 19-year old "rock-n-rollers" were not at all emotionally prepared for what they were going to experience in Vietnam, and that is why they were essentially "cannon fodder." The VC, on the other hand, were so committed to their cause that they could embrace, and even use, the terror that has burdened Willard and Kurtz with deep-seated guilt and doom.

Summary and Analysis of Chapter 1: Waiting in Saigon - Chapter 4: Search and Destroy

Summary

The sound of an approaching helicopter plays over a still frame showing a strip of palm trees in Vietnam. As the helicopter flies by, the first ominous notes of The Doors' "This is the End" begin. Then, the jungle landscape ignites in a series of explosions, filling the frame with dusty smoke and helicopters. Dissolve to an upside-down close-up of Captain Benjamin L. Willard, lying in bed, smoking a cigarette. The burning jungle fades in and out, layering fiery orange and red over Willard's paranoid eyes. As the sounds of the helicopter fade into the flutter of the ceiling fan, the camera pans over Willard's effects: booze, pills, and a handgun under his pillow. He jumps out of bed and peeks through the closed Venetian blinds onto the populated street. His gravelly voice-over states, "Saigon. Shit."

Willard's voice-over continues, as he describes always waking up and thinking he is back in the jungle. This is his second tour of duty, but after returning from Vietnam the first time, all he could think about was coming back. His wife divorced him and now he's in a Saigon hotel, waiting for his next assignment. The following moments play like a fever dream: Willard squats on the floor in his underwear, his face is painted, he punches his mirror and flips over his bed, bloodying his sheets. This man is at war with something - but it isn't Charlie.

Cut to two soldiers in silhouette, walking up the stairs to Willard's room. They have come to bring him to ComSec (Communications Security) intelligence in Nha Trang. Willard is so drunk that the soldiers have to physically throw him in the shower first. Cut to a helicopter landing in Nha Trang where a basic camp has been set up. In voice-over, Willard shares that this is the mission he has been waiting for, but also that it was his last. He continues to say that his story is intertwined with that of Col. Walter E. Kurtz.

Willard enters the trailer, where three soldiers are waiting for him, one of whom is General Corman. In close-up, Willard states for the record that he has never met any of the men before. Col. Lucas asks him questions about his history with the C.I.A. and ComSec I Corps, all of which he denies. Corman invites Willard to sit down for lunch. Lucas passes Willard a photograph, asking him if he has ever heard of Col. Walter E. Kurtz, an Operations Officer with the 5th Special Forces. Willard has, and the General asks Lucas to play "the tape." In a point-of-view shot, Willard looks down at the black-and-white photograph of a handsome, uniformed man with a furrowed brow. Kurtz's voice on the recording, though, sounds distant and wild. He talks of dreams and nightmares in a cold, haunting baritone. Willard's hands freeze as he listens to Kurtz describe assassinating pigs and cows - it sounds like the ramblings of a madman.

The General tells Willard that Kurtz was a brilliant Colonel and a good man, but soon after he joined the Special Forces, his actions and ideas became "unsound." Now, Kurtz is in Cambodia with a band of local followers who worship him like a god. Kurtz has also recently ordered the execution of Vietnamese intelligence agents he suspected of double-crossing him, so he is now wanted for murder. In intercut close-ups, the General ponders Kurtz's transformation - believing that Kurtz reached a breaking point and has gone insane. Lucas then tells Willard that his new - and highly classified - mission is to travel up the Nung River on a Navy Patrol Boat (or PBR, which means Patrol Boat, River), find the Colonel, and "Terminate his command." The other man at the table, a civilian who has been silent until now, elaborates, "Terminate. With extreme prejudice." Willard sits back in his chair, smoking a cigarette, and stares straight at the General.

Cut to an extreme wide shot of a helicopter flying over the rolling green hills. The music is psychedelic and menacing at the same time. From Willard's point of view, the camera skims over people working in rice fields. In voice-over, Willard contemplates how many people he has killed... "but this time, it [is] an American. And an officer." Cut to the Navy Patrol boat pulling away from the dock at sunset, as Willard wonders what he will do when he finds Kurtz. On the Patrol Boat, Willard is joined by a crew, which he describes as "rock-n-rollers with one foot in their graves": The Chef, Lance, Mr. Clean, and Phillips,"The Chief," who captains the boat. The Chief informs Willard that he brought one Captain Colby, Special Ops, up the Nung River, and he never returned. The Rolling Stones' "I Can't Get No... Satisfaction" plays on AVFM Radio while Willard looks through Kurtz's file. Lance waterskis behind the boat, and Mr. Clean dances.

A close-up of Kurtz's dossier reveals his exceptional achievements, and Willard cannot believe that this man is his target. Willard has trouble accepting that the voice he heard belonged to this man, who was on track to become a major military leader. Why would Kurtz, at 38 years old, leave that behind and pursue a transfer to Airborne Training? The sounds of a large explosion interrupt Willard's thoughts. The camera tracks along the side of the boat to show each crew member's reaction to the sound of the B-52 Strike. Smoke billows out of a destroyed village and Willard narrates that this is the Air Cavalry Division - 1st of the 9th, who are supposed to escort Willard and his crew to the mouth of the Nung River but apparently could not help themselves and had to bomb a village first. As the boat pulls into the shore, the camera tracks over a soldier tending to a Vietnamese mother holding a wounded baby in the chaos.

As a tank tears up rice paddies, a television crew captures the action and when Willard passes by, the director (played by Francis Ford Coppola) instructs him not to look into the camera. Willard trudges through the burning village looking for the Commanding Officer, shouting over the explosions and helicopters. He finds Captain Kilgore, a strapping man in a cowboy hat and aviator shades, who asks Willard and his crew to stand aside until the current activities are finished. With that, Kilgore opens a pack of playing cards and starts walking through the village, throwing individual cards on the (supposedly VC) corpses that litter the ground so that "Charlie" will know who committed the massacre. The soldiers help surviving women and children to safety, while a war photographer gathers visual evidence.

Kilgore comes across some of his soldiers standing over a wounded man who is using a pot lid to hold his intestines in. A Vietnamese-speaking soldier tells Kilgore that the man is just asking for water, and Kilgore shouts at the solider violently. He grabs his canteen and kneels low to the man, about to give him water, but then another soldier tells Kilgore that Lance Johnson, the famous surfer, happens to be on the PBR that just arrived. Kilgore stands, without giving any water to the wounded man, and walks towards Lance. Kilgore is a fan of Lance's surfing and introduces him to other surfers in the Cavalry. Willard smokes a cigarette and watches as a priest holds Holy Communion on the battlefield. A helicopter airlifts a cow out of the burning landscape.

Analysis

It is impossible to study *Apocalypse Now* without also learning about the turmoil that plagued the production. The film, a physical and metaphorical journey from sanity to madness, was similarly transformative for many of the creative forces involved, most notably Francis Ford Coppola, but also his leading man, Martin Sheen, who plays Capt. Willard. The dreamlike sequence that opens the film was shot on Sheen's 36th birthday, and Sheen, like his character, was completely drunk.

In his grizzled baritone, Willard (in voiceover) invites the audience into his mind, introducing the confessional nature of his narration. He reveals that he is battling some demons that have prevented him from returning to his pre-war life, though he never directly describes the atrocities he has seen. Instead, his paranoia and obsession are evidence enough. Sheen, who was fighting his own internal struggles at the time, went deep into Willard's soul while filming this scene. Willard's karate chop into the mirror and the resulting blood are real. When Sheen started bleeding, Coppola asked the actor if he wanted to stop rolling and Sheen insisted that they continue. The scotch is real, too, as is the shower that sobers him up. The emotions caught on film are real, which heightens the immediacy of the performances and the film.

The General's quarters at Nha Trang, where Willard receives his orders to kill Col. Kurtz, looks like an archetypal American living room rather than a trailer in the middle of the jungle. Col. Lucas questions Willard about missions he has undertaken in the past, missions that he is not supposed to discuss - but we learn that he worked for the CIA and has likely been involved in a sanctioned assassination before (besides what he may have seen and done in his first tour of Vietnam). Kurtz and Willard are both killers, except they are on opposite sides of the law - and this was the contradiction at the heart of the Vietnam War. American troops killed millions of

Vietnamese civilians in an effort to contain the spread of communism in the Cold War era. In the process, they turned thousands of American soldiers into killers, and more than 50,000 of them into victims. In the thick of it, soldiers had a hard time figuring out who they were supposed to be killing, and why.

Willard narrates that this assignment took him deep into hell. Similarly, the Vietnam War brought out the worst in the previously infallible American psyche, the kind of jingoistic patriotism that Kurtz himself once embraced. "It was no accident," Willard says about his being assigned to find Kurtz, "there was no way to tell his [Kurtz's] story without telling my own. If his story is a confession, than so is mine." We know from this moment that through his association with Kurtz, Willard will come to terms with his own internal darkness over the course of the film. During the trip upriver, Willard starts reading Kurtz's dossier and learns more and more about the man he is being sent to kill, and as a result, starts to understand what made him snap.

Simultaneously, as the PBR travels along the river, Willard's crew (and the audience) witnesses increasingly shocking atrocities, some of which would drive any person to the brink. Coppola never intended to structure *Apocalypse Now* as a political statement - his motivations were to create something far more visceral. He said, "What I hoped for was to take the audience through an unprecedented experience of war and have them react as much as those who had gone through the war" (Cowie 121).

Arguably, the most memorable character Willard encounters is Col. Kilgore. John Milius often compared *Apocalypse Now* to another epic tale: *The Odyssey*. In that context, Kilgore is Cyclops, a destructive monster. In many ways, Kilgore is modeled after a real-life American hero: John Wayne, down to his cowboy hat and scarf. He is an archetype of American masculinity, and although his unflinching confidence makes him a great soldier, it was men like Kilgore who powered the "remorseless machine" through Vietnam (Cowie 137). He engages in battle with such gusto that he never stops to question the larger moral implication of his actions. Coppola also manages a tongue-in-cheek cameo in this section of the film, as the newsreel director instructing Willard to "go on through...just like in the war." In this moment, Willard looks back at Coppola with shock on his face - his expression embodies the question that many Americans asked themselves during the Vietnam War: "What exactly are we doing here?"

Summary and Analysis of Chapter 5: Beach Party - Chapter 8: The Tiger in the Jungle

Summary

The camera tracks slowly along the darkened beach, where the soldiers have congregated around makeshift fires, drinking beer and eating steak. Willard, in voice-over, calls it a "beach party," and the camera stops to show Col. Kilgore holding court with an acoustic guitar, surrounded by soldiers. Willard comments that Kilgore has a "weird light around him" because he knew nothing was going to happen to him in Vietnam. Sure enough, Kilgore seems entirely confident to the point that he believes himself to be invincible. Willard tries to get Kilgore's attention, pointing out on the map the two entry points into the Nung River. At first, Kilgore pokes fun at Willard's seriousness and comments that it's a Viet Cong stronghold, but then, Mike comments that the entry point is a great spot for surfing. Suddenly unconcerned that this particular area is "hairy," Kilgore stands at attention, ready for the mission. To the detractor who claims that their destination is controlled by the Viet Cong, Kilgore exclaims, "Charlie don't surf!"

The next morning, Kilgore strides confidently out of the jungle, leading the rest of Air Cavalry 9's soldiers towards their helicopters. The trumpet sounds out as the helicopters take off into the dusty dawn light. Willard's PBR, meanwhile, is being airlifted to its next destination. Dissolve to a sequence of the helicopters flying over what looks like a serene tropical paradise, with Willard's contemplative profile layered over the frame. Meanwhile, Kilgore keeps discussing the topic he is most interested in - surfing. He asks Lance what kind of surfboard he uses (note that there is a surfboard attached to the underside of Kilgore's helicopter). Then, Kilgore commands one of his men to put on the music - he claims that when he plays Wagner during an attack, it scares his intended victims. *Ride of the Valkyries* comes on - very loud. Willard looks mildly amused.

Cut to a placid courtyard where a young Vietnamese girl prepares greens to sell at market. The sound of children singing emerges from a small schoolhouse on the other side of the courtyard a group of uniformed children come outside. The serenity is interrupted by the sound of helicopters and Wagner from overhead. The teachers hurry the children to safety and residents of the village begin to panic. The helicopters fly in a V-shaped attack formation and start firing. Viet Cong jump out of the bushes and prepare to return fire. Kilgore's crew blows up several homes. The village erupts in gunfire and black smoke. A vehicle loaded with Viet Cong tries to cross over a rickety bridge, but the Air Cav fires and blows the bridge - and the car - to smithereens. Meanwhile, a few of the helicopters land and the American soldiers storm the village on foot. One soldier is shot in the leg, and others attend to him. He lies in the courtyard, screaming for mercy. Kilgore orders the wounded to be taken to the hospital, and his men to get out of the village.

Orange smoke starts to rise into the sky - napalm. A village woman throws a live grenade into the grounded helicopter, so Kilgore follows her in his helicopter and shoots her down. Simultaneously, Kilgore points out the waves to Lance. He lands his helicopter - which has "Death From Above" emblazoned on the front. Willard stumbles through the orange smoke as explosions echo around him. The PBR appears, having been airlifted by one of the Air Cav helicopters. Kilgore sends two of his men to surf the waves while gunfire is still strafing the water. Willard tries to tell Kilgore that it is too dangerous to surf but Kilgore is determined. He stands up out of the trench and rips his shirt off. He calls a squad of fighter jets and orders a napalm attack, promising Lance that they will "clean this place up." The jets appear in the sky and suddenly, the village explodes in a neat row of fiery orange clouds. Kilgore watches triumphantly and proclaims, "I love the smell of napalm in the morning!" Behind him, Vietnamese villagers file out of what used to be their home, heads hung low.

In the evening, Willard and his crew are back on the PBR, and the village is still burning around them as they set off on their way. They get high and Willard comments in his voice-over that the boys just want to get through this and go home. Willard says, though, that he has been back and "home doesn't exist anymore." Taking a swig of booze, Willard wonders that if Kilgore is considered to be playing by the rules, why is the US Army after Kurtz? How was Kurtz's infraction so much worse than Kilgore's senseless brutality? Dissolve to the stoned Chef rambling on about mangoes, before deciding to disembark and go look for some. Willard, concerned, accompanies him. They walk together through the dense jungle, the leafy ferns often obscuring them in the frame. Willard asks Chef about his nickname, and Chef responds that he is actually a real chef. He was about to go to school in Paris to become a saucier when he got drafted.

In a wide shot, the two men creep through the vast jungle. Suddenly, Willard becomes quiet and his ears perk up. The Chef stops rambling, knowing something is wrong. They tread carefully into the trees, guns locked and loaded. All of a sudden - a tiger jumps out of the trees. Chef runs away, screaming psychotically. Willard fires a few shots at the tiger and follows closely behind. The crew, alarmed, pulls the boat away, thinking that Charlie had been hiding in the bushes. Chef, however, is in a panicked state, screaming about the tiger and sobbing. He cries, "All I want to do is fucking cook, man!" He keeps repeating the mantra, "never get out of the boat!" Willard watches the younger man fall apart, his face stony as always. In his voice-over, he comments, "Never get out of the boat, unless you're going all the way." Kurtz got off the boat, Willard continues, "he split from the whole fucking program". Willard wonders what Kurtz saw during his first tour that sent him in such a radical direction.

Late at night, Willard uses a flashlight to keep studying Kurtz's file. He ponders what Kurtz's family and friends thought when he decided that instead of continuing on a path towards becoming a General, he'd rather join the Green Berets. Willard remembers his own time at boot camp, saying that at 19 the course nearly killed him. He labels Kurtz "a tough motherfucker." Dissolve to Chef, who dictates the letter he is writing to "Eva" about his encounter with the tiger. He writes that he does not know where they are going on his mission. Meanwhile, Willard reads about Kurtz's decision to carry out Operation Arcangel in October 1967, which was a major success. He never had official clearance to carry out the mission, and almost got sacked for his rebellion - but then the press got a hold of it and instead, Kurtz was promoted to Colonel. Willard comments, "what balls." At that point, the boat goes around a bend in the river and bright lights are shining from the land. Loud music is playing, and American soldiers are setting up a large, camouflage-patterned stage surrounded by bleachers. Mr. Clean comments on how bizarre the scene is. They go to shore, and find themselves at Hau Phat, where there is a well-stocked American Army supply warehouse.

Coppola's signature tracking shot follows Willard and his crew towards the busy warehouse. The sergeant in charge asks Mr. Clean and Chef to state their destination, but they obviously can't because they don't know what it is. Willard steps in and tells the sergeant to hand over the supplies anyway, because the mission is classified. The Sergeant sneers and asks the crew to move along. Willard, not willing to take "no" for an answer, slams the man down onto the desk. He quickly changes his tune, directing Chef and Mr. Clean towards the supply storage. He offers Willard and his crew press box seats for the show - apparently, some Playboy Bunnies will be performing for the troops.

Summary

One of the most famous sequences in *Apocalypse Now* (and one of the most difficult to execute) is Col. Kilgore leading the Air Cavalry 9 to attack a village at Vin Din Drop, so that Willard and his crew can safely reach the mouth of the Nung River. Kilgore celebrates the grandiosity of war by providing a soundtrack for systematic killing. Peter Cowie writes, "by presenting Kilgore's exploits in operatic terms, Coppola suggests the self-conceit and the fascination with pyrotechnics that kept the Americans from challenging the Viet Cong successfully at a guerilla level" (Cowie 138). In fact, throughout *Apocalypse Now*, the audience rarely sees more than a fleeting close-up of "the enemy," which is an accurate representation of the way many American troops felt about Charlie's guerilla tactics. This is part of the film's subjective nature, which draws the viewer into the experience of the soldiers - who don't seem to know whom they are fighting against and what they are fighting for.

Kilgore, for all his bravado, does not know the answers to these questions either, but he does not care enough to ask. He balks at the prospect of escorting Willard and his crew into Vin Din Drop until he hears that it's a great place for surfing. This is enough to fire Kilgore up. Unlike Willard and Kurtz, Kilgore does not ask philosophical questions, but chooses to remain focused on constantly asserting his power. He, too, appears to have gone insane - but his madness is sanctioned, forcing

Willard to ponder if there is any real difference between Kilgore - his ally - and Kurtz, his enemy. No matter what Willard may have done while behind the mask of war, he can identify the tragedy unfolding before him, when he comments, "we'd cut 'em in half with a machine gun and offer 'em a band-aid."

Meanwhile, Willard's crew members each embody a different perspective, making the PBR a microcosm of the war itself. Chief follows orders and obeys the army's hierarchy, just as he has been taught. Even though he knows there is something suspicious about Willard's mission, he does as he is told. Lance represents the psychedelic drug culture that pervaded the war (and the *Apocalypse Now* set). Mr. Clean, (played by a 14-year old Laurence Fishburne), is essentially a child, just as many of the soldiers who were drafted to go to Vietnam were barely out of high school. It would be just as easy to imagine him dancing to the Rolling Stones at a school dance rather than on a Navy Patrol Boat. Chef, however, is the conscience of the crew, a distinction that clouds him in an aura of doom. He talks about his girlfriend and his dreams of being a saucier. He innocently goes out for mangoes and ends up being nearly attacked by a tiger.

The hypocrisy of Kilgore serves to deepen Willard's understanding of Kurtz. He describes Kurtz's unauthorized mission, "Operation Arcangel," which nearly cost him his job - until the press deemed it a success, and Kurtz was promoted instead. Willard admires Kurtz's "balls" for taking matters into his own hands, commenting that he, too, is tired of the lies. Kurtz was promoted simply so that the army could save face and trumpet a successful mission, meaning that Kurtz had "gotten off the boat" once before, and was rewarded for it. The root of the problem is now that Kurtz has escaped from the American grasp, both literally and metaphorically. His dossier proves to unearth many of the lies surrounding the American presence in Vietnam - and once all the politics have been stripped away, all that remains is darkness and death.

When the PBR arrives at Hau Phat, Coppola demonstrates the excesses of war and the physical size of the American effort. The supply warehouse is fully stocked, and the soldiers can get whatever they want, even "Panama Red" (a type of marijuana). Mr. Clean is shocked at the outrageous setup, commenting how bizarre it is to see the USO stage erected in the middle of a war zone. The soldiers stationed at Hau Phat, meanwhile, seem far less concerned about life or death, but rather, they are stressed out about the upcoming performance. This display - the supplies, the drugs, the Playboy Bunnies - these are the band-aids that America gave its soldiers, hoping to keep their patriotism alive while they risked their lives to fight an invisible enemy.

Summary and Analysis of Chapter 9: Entertaining the Boys - Chapter 12 : Do Lung Bridge

Summary

The blinding light of a helicopter cuts through the night sky, drowning out the soldiers' whooping cheers. The helicopter, which bears the Playboy Bunny symbol, lands on a landing pad decorated with stars and stripes in the center of the open-air amphitheater. The Promoter jumps out of the helicopter, grabs the mic, and congratulates the soldiers on "Operation Brute Force." Then, three scantily-clad Playboy bunnies pop out of the helicopter and start gyrating for the jubilant crowd. The Playmate of the Year does a provocative solo dance, while rubbing her nose as if she's been snorting cocaine. The camera pans across a group of Vietnamese onlookers (some of them children) watching the spectacle from behind a chain link fence.

At first, the Playboy Bunnies seem to be enjoying the attention, flirting and taunting the men. However, the crowd starts to get a little rowdy, and suddenly, a group of soldiers storms the stage. The Promoter rushes the frightened girls into the helicopter and drops smoke bombs to dissipate the crowd. Willard watches the scene, placidly amused. As the helicopter takes off, two soldiers hang onto its landing skids. The pilot is able to shake the men into the decorative pool before departing. In his voiceover, Willard comments that Charlie never gets USO.

Cut to daylight. A helicopter hovers over the messy remnants of the night's performance as the PBR returns to its route. Willard comments that the people running this war are "four star clowns." Their boat passes another PBR, and the passing sailors moon Willard's crew and throw a smoke grenade onto the roof of the boat, which promptly catches fire. Later, Lance and Chef repair the roof with palm fronds. Willard goes back to Kurtz's dossier in a medium shot with Clean drumming away in the foreground.

Willard leafs through photographs of Kurtz's camp in the highlands - which had become a frequent target of ambushes, leading him to order the assassination of the South Vietnamese Army Colonels. Indeed, after that, Willard observes, there were no more enemy strikes on Kurtz. Close-up on Willard's eyes to transition into a flashback of his meeting with General Corman back in Saigon. In an extreme close-up, the camera glides over Corman's hands, his voice dreamily dissonant over Willard's thoughts. Willard comments that the army tried to bring Kurtz back to the fold, but "they lost him - he was gone." Willard comments that the VC is scared of Kurtz and will not touch him.

Clean keeps drumming, which is clearly annoying Willard, who complains to Phillips. Phillips says that Clean has been on the boat for 7 months and alludes to the fact that the young man does not particularly like Capt. Willard, either. Then, Phillips comments that he is doing his job by taking Willard up the river to a classified location, and he won't ask where they are going - but he knows that their location is going to be "hot." In alternating close-ups, Willard tells Phillips that their destination is "about 75 clicks above the Do Lung Bridge." Phillips is silent, digesting the information before stating that Willard is asking him to go to Cambodia - where Americans are not supposed to be. Willard promises that if Phillips can get him close to the destination, he'll cut the crew loose and go on by himself.

Cut to a wide shot of the boat taking a bend in the river, accompanied by menacing score. Dissolve to an extreme close-up of Willard's eye. He starts reading a letter that Kurtz wrote to his son. Cut to a close-up of the neatly typed letter in Willard's hands in which Kurtz tells his son that he has been accused of murder. Dissolve to a bird's eye view of the boat, dwarfed by the dense, leafy jungle on both sides of the river. In his letter, Kurtz claims that the Vietnamese men and woman he executed were actually proven double agents and calls the charges against him "insane." He claims that his ruthlessness is only a symptom of his clarity and he is a victim of the American Army's timid morality. The PBR passes by the burning carcass of a helicopter in a tree, lighting up the sky. Meanwhile, Chef and Clean get into a shouting match and Lance paints his face with camouflage makeup. Willard examines the most recent photo of Kurtz - which is a shot of him from behind, broad shoulders and bald head.

The PBR crosses paths with a Vietnamese sampan. Phillips insists on stopping the boat and searching it to make sure that it is not trafficking supplies for the VC. Willard tries to talk Phillips out of doing this, but the Chief is a stickler for following orders. He commands Chef to search every corner of the sampan, and notices that a woman is sitting on a woven basket rather protectively. Suddenly, Mr. Clean opens fire and kills everyone on the boat. Chef, rattled, opens the basket and finds that the woman was trying to protect a tiny yellow puppy. Lance takes the puppy and keeps it. Then, the crew realizes that the Vietnamese woman is still alive and Phillips commands Chef to bring her on board so that they can find her some medical help. Willard strongly disagrees and nonchalantly shoots her. The sun hangs low in the sky and the crew silently prepares to move on. Fade to black.

The PBR cuts through the silent water in the evening light. In his voiceover, Willard says that the whole Vietnam war is based on lies. He also muses that his crew will never look at him the same way again. Cut to a close-up on Willard's face in the darkness, as he says he now knows things about Kurtz that are not in the dossier. The boat approaches the Do Lung Bridge, the last army outpost on the Nung River. Flares shatter all around it, and Lance calls it beautiful. He reveals to Chef that he is tripping on acid. As the PBR gets closer to the bridge, American soldiers dive into the water, suitcases in hand, begging to be taken home. Remnants of charred helicopters litter the shore. Then, a voice calls out from the darkness, asking for

Captain Willard.

Lieutenant Carlson has been waiting for the PBR for three days. He has been sent from the Trang with a delivery for Willard and mail for the boat. He describes the Do Lung Bridge as "the asshole of the world." Willard quickly disembarks and says he is going to look for some information. Lance follows him into the darkness and Chief pulls the boat away, saying he will meet up with them on the other side of the bridge. Light bounces off the guns and helmets, creating distorted shadows. Lance and Willard creep along the coast in silhouette, taking in the desperation around them - agonizing screams, artillery fire, explosions in the water. They jump into a trench, where the soldiers are screaming and pushing each other like lunatics. No one is making any sense, and there is clearly nobody in charge here. The soldiers in the trench just stare at Willard and Lance like they are bats hanging from the wall.

Lance, meanwhile, has brought his puppy with him, cuddled in his jacket. He climbs up out of the trench and observes the destruction until Willard commands him to come down. One soldier is firing his machine gun into the darkness, trying to kill "the gooks on the wire." He can hear a Viet Cong soldier screaming, "Fuck you, G.I.!" from under a pile of bodies, and keeps firing in the direction of that sound. He fetches another soldier named Roach who manages to locate the sound and eliminate it. When Willard asks Roach if he knows who is in command, Roach simply replies, "yeah" and walks away, disappearing into the darkness. Back on the boat, Clean tells Phillips that two men have just been blown off the bridge. Willard and Lance return to the boat with ammunition - having given up on finding a commanding officer, Willard decides that it is time to keep going and find Kurtz. Phillips questions Willard's decision but Willard has his mind set on continuing up the river. The American flag on the top of the PBR waves forlornly in the wind as the boat pulls away form the shore. The Do Lung bridge starts to collapse - Charlie has been successful for now - but the Americans will rebuild it the next day and the cycle will continue. Fade to black.

Analysis

The Playboy Bunny sequence is one of the few instances where female characters appear in *Apocalypse Now*. It is an appropriate representation of the war, though. For these soldiers, "women... exist only in photographs," writes Peter Cowie (139). The Playboy Bunnies, however, are simply those photographs come to life, hence the frenzy that erupts midway through the show. To these men, the Bunnies are not as much real people as they are symbols of America and the comforts of home. They are reminders of the fact that most of these soldiers, like the men on Willard's PBR, are very young and not quite sure what they are fighting for. And yet, all they keep hearing is that their mission in Vietnam is important. Coppola wanted this scene to be bizarre and detached from reality, which adds to his cynical perspective on the war itself. To that end, the set is completely over-the-top, and the bleachers are flanked with phallic symbols.

The Promoter congratulates the soldiers on "Operation Brute Force," also known as "Operation Speedy Express," which took place from Dec. 1968 - May 1969. The mission was supposedly intended to sever the VC's supply lines to Cambodia. It later became the subject of intense public scrutiny when the media alleged that less than half of the reported 10,000 Vietnamese victims were actually Viet Cong. Meanwhile, 40 American soldiers died in the process. The obsession with "body count" and "kill ratio" continued to plague the military, as American citizens became more and more skeptical as to whether or not their loved ones (and tax dollars) were actually accomplishing anything in Vietnam. "While the US Government managed to conceal some of its operations from the public at home, most of the horror appeared nightly on American television" (Cowie 142).

Coppola continues to portray the practice of unchecked violence with the massacre on the Sampan, which was the director's response to the real-life My Lai Massacre, one of the most maniacal displays of American military brutality in history. On March 16, 1968, 105 members of Charlie Company, a unit of the American Division's 11th Light Infantry Brigade, stormed into the South Vietnamese village of My Lai and systematically murdered over 500 innocent men, women, and children over the course of 4 hours. In addition, the soldiers raped, sodomized and mutilated many of their victims. It turned out that there was not a single VC among them. Vietnam, and My Lai in particular, suddenly changed the image of soldiers in America. Were they heroes...or criminals? Was My Lai the exception, or was it the norm? Soldiers who participated in the attack describe feeling like they were losing their minds.

Similarly, Mr. Clean opens fire on the Sampan for no real reason. Afterwards, he looks more confused than anything. Meanwhile, the lines of morality have become blurry, even for the steadfast Chief. Although he is the one responsible for pulling over the sampan in the first place, he wants to take the injured woman to get help, but Willard, who is more focused on getting to Kurtz at this point, kills her in cold blood. This dichotomy is similar to the divide between Kurtz and Kilgore. One man, (Mr. Clean) kills innocents because he thinks it is his purpose, and another (Willard) kills an innocent woman because he doesn't want to deal with her. And yet - both actions, despite the motivation behind them, result in the death of innocents. This scene is a microcosm of the My Lai massacre.

The sense of confusion reaches its peak once the PBR arrives at the Do Lung Bridge, where no one has any clue who is in charge, and morale is nonexistent. The place reeks of desperation. Vittorio Storaro says that the dim, shadowy lighting was a result of the fact that they never had enough artificial light to illuminate the jungle, leading his crew to rely on the intermittent explosions as light sources. However, the dark, murky atmosphere makes the Do Lung Bridge feel like a place that everyone else has forgotten about. Night after night, Charlie blows up the bridge, and day after day, the Americans build it back up. This futile, Sisyphean cycle is representative of the fact that the American Army seemed to lose control of the war, while publicly scrambling to keep selling it to citizens back home.

While Willard is scrambling around the trenches looking for a C.O, Lance is tripping on acid, clutching a puppy to his chest. Both Coppola and Milius believed that the American Army's dependence on drugs in Vietnam was part of the reason for the eventual capitulation, and so the drug culture is abundant in *Apocalypse Now*. Peter Cowie shares the results of a Pentagon study, which estimated that "nearly 30% of American soldiers in Vietnam had taken either opium or heroin" (147). These psychedelic extracurricular activities ended up extending beyond the screenplay and onto Coppola's set. Most of his cast and crew were indulging in some form of mind-altering substances, including, apparently, some of the Filipino helicopter pilots. The chaotic atmosphere of the film reflects both the circumstances of the war, and of the shoot itself.

Summary and Analysis of Chapter 13: Mr. Clean's Death - Chapter 15: Kurtz's Compound

Summary

It's daytime. The camera tilts up from the murky water to the PBR as it makes its lonely way upriver. Chef distributes the mail to the different sailors, who all sit and happily read missives from home. Willard, meanwhile, opens the letter that Carlson delivered to him at Do Lung Bridge. It is an official memo from the Army and says that Captain Richard Colby, the last man who had been sent to find Kurtz, was not MIA as previously reported - he has actually defected and is now Kurtz's follower. Included in the package is proof - the letter that Colby sent to his wife after arriving at Kurtz's compound. It reads (in a hasty pencil scrawl), "Sell the house - Sell the car - Sell the kids- Find someone else - Forget it - I'm never coming back!"

Meanwhile, Chef opens his package from Eva, which includes a newspaper clipping about the Manson Family murders. Lance, who now appears to be permanently tripped out, lights a purple flare and dances around the boat, calling the colorful smoke a "Purple Haze." Clean listens to a taped message from his mother on a portable cassette player. Suddenly, shots come firing out of the jungle towards the boat. The crew starts firing into the woods at their hidden enemy. Clean is hit. After the gunfire ceases, Clean's contorted body remains sprawled across the back of the boat. Lance grumbles that his dog has gone missing. Chief, in a rare show of emotion, weeps over Clean's body. The dead man's mother continues to speak on the cassette player, saying that she wants grandchildren to love and spoil before saying her farewell, reminding her son to "stay out of the way of bullets." Chief breaks down.

Later, the boat continues up the river quietly - bathed in the misty evening light. The pall of death lies over the crew as they pass under the fuselage of a wrecked airplane. The mist becomes thick and milky, enveloping the boat. Voices are audible from the shore and Chief wants to stop the boat because he cannot see, but Willard insists that he continue. Chef is wild with paranoia, and Lance howls madly into the fog. Willard's gaze is intense and in voiceover, he says, "he was close. He was real close." Suddenly, the air clears and a flurry of arrows comes flying out of the woods, hailing down onto the boat. Chief tries to steer away from the shore. Willard tries to stop Chef and Lance from opening fire, saying that the arrows are harmless little sticks, but they don't listen. Lance breaks an arrow in half and puts it on his head.

Chief screams at Willard for leading them into this mess, grabs his gun, and starts shooting at their hidden assailants. Suddenly, Chief stops, stunned, and stumbles backwards. The camera tilts down to show an arrowhead piercing Chief's heart as he starts bleeding from the mouth. He whispers, "a spear," and then falls, but Willard catches him and tries to hold his head up. Chief summons every ounce of strength he has left and wraps his hands tightly around Willard's throat. Willard presses his palm into the dying man's face in an act of self-defense - until Chief bleeds out. After the attack is over, Willard finally reveals the true nature of the mission to Chef, who explodes with anger. Lance cradles Chief's body in the river while Chef screams at Willard about the absurdity of a mission into Cambodia to kill an American colonel. Finally, Chef tells Willard that he and Lance will accompany him to Kurtz's compound, but only if they stay on the boat. Cut to a close-up on Lance's dreamy face as he emerges from the water, while Chief's body slips below the surface.

The boat moves on through the night, guided by flaming torches burning along the shore. Dissolve to daylight, and in a dreamy, menacing sequence, the boat passes a ceremonial arrangement of human skulls arranged on a small inlet. In his voiceover, Willard admits that he was afraid about what he was going to find at the end of his journey. He rips up Kurtz's dossier and leaves the shredded documents floating in the water. Cut to a high angle shot of Willard looking at something through his binoculars. He tells Chef to keep moving and instructs Lance to keep his hands away from his gun. Cut to the angle from behind Willard, who is facing dozens of painted-white people floating on flat canoes in the water. They stand perfectly still and silent - and the only score is a bass playing a single note over and over. Chef inches the PBR forward and the smaller boats separate to let it pass through.

Even Willard looks nervous as the PBR pulls up the shore. Hundreds of Kurtz's Montagnard followers, all armed, stand silently on the temple steps and hilly landscape, waiting. Suddenly, an American male voice breaks the spell. "It's all right! It's all right! It's all been approved!", he shouts, flailing wildly from within the stationary crowd. Chef hesitates because those "bastards" have attacked the boat once already. The American tells him to sound his siren, and Chef does. Everyone scatters except for the Photojournalist, who meets the PBR as it docks. There is a naked corpse dangling from a tree above the water as the Photojournalist shakes the crew's hands and asks Chef for a cigarette. The Photojournalist says that all of Kurtz's "children" have gathered because they are afraid that Willard has come to take Kurtz away. Willard says that he just wants to talk to Kurtz. The Photojournalist leads Willard and Chef inland, sputtering a stream of consciousness about Kurtz's grand vision. The temple grounds are littered with corpses.

Willard spots Captain Colby with blood on his hands, surrounded by children. In a close-up, Willard searches Colby's eyes for recognition but is met by his blank, empty stare. The Photojournalist leads Willard through the crowd to the base of a flight of stone stairs leading into the temple where Kurtz resides. It is covered in human heads. The Photojournalist apologetically admits that sometimes Kurtz "goes too far." He says that Kurtz has gone out into the jungle with his people. Chef tells Willard that they should return to the boat and Willard agrees. Cut back to Lance, who is perched on the side of the boat, folded into a squat. He shoots down the body hanging from the tree. Inside the boat, their faces obscured in shadows, Chef calls Kurtz "wacko" and "evil" and describes what they have seen as "pagan idolatry."

Chef agrees to assist Willard on his mission to kill Kurtz - anything to get out of here. Willard instructs Chef to wait on the boat while he and Lance go to land to find the Colonel. If they do not return by 2200 hours, Willard tells Chef to radio in an airstrike on the compound.

The rain pours down on Lance and Willard as they walk onto the land. In Willard's voiceover, he says that Kurtz had clearly gone insane. He describes the dead bodies around the compound as "North Vietnamese, Viet Cong, and Cambodian," proof of the fact that Kurtz was waging his own war. Willard is aware of the fact that he is only alive because Kurtz has allowed it. Then, a crowd of Kurtz's "children" is upon him. They shove him to the ground, dragging him around in the mud, and the camera makes a full circle to capture his desperate expression as he succumbs to them. Lance just looks on stupidly.

Willard is led inside the darkened temple in handcuffs, with sharp streaks of light defining his silhouette. In his voiceover, he describes the smell inside as "slow death, malaria, and nightmares." He is taken into a small room and forced at gunpoint to kneel down. From the shadows of a small canopy, an American voice asks him where he is from. This, at last, is Col. Kurtz. The camera tracks in close, but only Kurtz's hands and bald head are visible. He sounds perfectly sane as he describes his travels on the Ohio River. Willard gives him a sidelong glance, unsure how to respond. Kurtz takes a bowl of water into his lap and splashes it onto his face and his shiny scalp.

Then, Kurtz's eyes finally shine out from the darkness like a wild tiger waiting to pounce. Willard says that he has been sent on a classified mission. Kurtz asks Willard if he thinks he (Kurtz) is insane and if his methods unsound. Willard boldly replies that he sees no method at all. Kurtz asks Willard, point blank, if he is an assassin. His full face catches the light, and Willard proclaims that he is a soldier. Kurtz focuses his glassy eyes on Willard and decrees that he is neither soldier nor assassin. He is "an errand boy sent by grocery clerks to collect the bill."

Analysis

Coppola invokes the American cultural context of the era by peppering *Apocalypse Now* with timely musical choices. The opening section and the ending of *Apocalypse Now* play out against *This is the End* by The Doors. The Doors rose to fame in the late 1960s, and were a major part of the soundtrack for the psychedelic drug culture, enhanced by lead singer Jim Morrison's onstage antics and well-publicized substance abuse. Originally, Coppola had wanted to use The Doors' music for the score of the entire film, but it just didn't feel right. Sound editor Walter Murch says, "There was no connection other than a very deep bond between the psyche of Jim Morrison and the psyche of this film" (Cowie 101). The Doors' music embodied the rebellion, alienation, drugs, and hedonism that came to define the popular youth culture of the 1960s and 70s.

Later, Lance mentions "Purple Haze," which is a Jimi Hendrix song from 1967. The term "Purple Haze" refers to LSD. The Rolling Stones' "I Can't Get No Satisfaction," which Mr. Clean dances to at the beginning of the PBR's journey, was released in 1965 and refers to sexual frustration. Figures like Jim Morrison, Jimi Hendrix, Keith Richards, and Mick Jagger were heroes to young men like the crew of Willard's PBR - they were representatives of the counter-culture, which is in direct ideological conflict with the American presence in Vietnam. However, in the context of the jungle, their music and the ideologies it connotes can only comfort these men - it can't save them.

These pop culture references also allow the audience to understand the world these young soldiers have left behind. They have come to Vietnam with the promise of becoming heroes, but many of them, like Clean and Chef, lack any kind of emotional connection to their mission. They just want to get home and do the things that 18-20 year old American men liked to do: chase girls, listen to music, maybe do some drugs, and surf. Willard even describes them as "...just kids, rock and rollers with one foot in their graves." By contrast, Willard is jaded. He knows from experience that Vietnam won't go away even when these kids get back home. He is on this journey to find Kurtz, yes, but he is also on this journey in order to face the darkest parts of himself. He is the commander of this mission because he has something to prove, while his crew are just passengers. Once Chief realizes this, he tries to retaliate - but it's too late.

In his early notes, Coppola wrote, *Apocalypse Now* "is made of four basic units or elements: FIRE (night bombing), WATER (the beach and the river), AIR (wind of helicopter and monsoon), and EARTH (mud, holes, bomb crater, green foliage" (Cowie 34). As the film reaches its climax, the scenery is more reminiscent of the "Earth" category, especially at Kurtz's compound, which appears to be growing up naturally out of the ground. The boat passes under the shells of helicopters and planes, indicating that these war machines are no match for what lies deep in the jungle. The evil is much more deep-seated, as Coppola wrote in his version of a synopsis for the film:

> As our protagonist travels through the insanities and absurdities of the American involvement in the war, he is more and more drawn to the jungle itself, its primeval mystique and immense power. It becomes clear that the American war 'to bring civilization to the ignorant millions' is merely the extension of mercantile colonialism and that the horror and savagery lie not in the jungle, but in the American culture itself, with its powerless [sic] technology and pop culture (Cowie 35).

As the PBR gets closer and closer to Kurtz, casualties befall the small crew. All of these characters fit into common war film tropes: Mr. Clean is the young upstart who requires protection from his stronger comrades, Chief is the hardened soldier with a heart of gold who plays by the rules, Chef is the sensitive soul always on the verge of a breakdown, and Lance exists in his own world. In their metaphorical journey into the Heart of Darkness, only Willard and Lance survive. The other three would never have been able to emerge from Kurtz's compound alive, simply because they never would have been able to understand Kurtz well enough to conquer him. Willard, meanwhile, sees himself in Kurtz and makes a conscious decision to travel the opposite path. Lance, on the other hand, becomes so pliable that he loses the ability to differentiate between good and evil. He is a follower, not a leader, and only leaves Kurtz's compound because Willard drags him back to the PBR.

Summary and Analysis of Chapter 16 : Interrogation - Chapter 20: End Credits

Summary

In a low angle shot, the Photojournalist climbs up the temple stairs through the overgrown jungle. He shoves dead bodies out of his way as he approaches the bamboo cage where Willard has been imprisoned. The Photojournalist gives the weak, bloodied Willard a sip of water and a drag of his cigarette. He asks Willard why a nice guy like him would want to kill a genius. He makes sure that Willard knows that Kurtz has something in mind for him. Willard looks him dead in the eyes, and the Photojournalist keeps ranting. In a close-up one-shot through the bamboo bars, the Photojournalist shares his belief that Kurtz is dying and "hates all of this."

Back on the boat, Chef tries to get some sleep under his poncho while the rain pours down - before he realizes that it's past 2200 hours. Cut to a wide shot of the PBR, with the sound of Chef calling Trang. Cut to a close-up of a man's feet walking along the muddy ground in the rain. In a point of view shot, Willard is draped weakly over the side of his bamboo cage like an animal, his face green and muddy. He looks up into the camera and opens his eyes wide, coming face to face with Kurtz, who is in full camouflage makeup. They lock eyes in alternating close-ups - Kurtz is shot from a low angle and Willard is shot from a high angle. Kurtz turns and walks away and a hand reaches out of the darkness to drop an object on Willard's lap. A close-up reveals that it is Chef's severed head. Willard screams in disgust and shakes it to the ground. He starts to weep.

Dissolve to the dawn, tilt down from the heavens to a bird's-eye-view of Kurtz's compound. Two men carry a weakened Willard through the temple corridor and lay him on a mat on the floor. A man holds his head up while a woman ladles water into his mouth. In a close-up, Willard struggles to move his head, but refuses to eat even a spoonful of rice. He turns his face towards camera and in his point-of-view shot, he sees Kurtz's shadow moving around nearby. Coppola creates the interaction between the men using a series of dissolves. An armed soldier stands guard. Kurtz waits. Willard smokes a cigarette. Kurtz catches a fly. Smoke swirls around the stone idols in the temple. Then, Kurtz's voice cuts through the silence and he starts reciting poetry. Willard now has the strength to sit up to look at him. Meanwhile, the Photojournalist leans on Willard's lap, rambling about physics and love. Kurtz looks up and hurls something at the Photojournalist, who becomes silent for a moment, and then gets up and leaves. Kurtz looks over at Willard before turning back to his book.

In his voiceover, Willard admits that he has no idea what to do. He is free to go but cannot seem to leave. He concludes that Kurtz knows more about what Willard will do than Willard himself. He surveys Kurtz's effects in point-of-view close-ups, the camera moving over his military uniform, his medals, and photographs of his wife and son. Willard wonders how Kurtz's family and former colleagues would react if they knew how far Kurtz had gone. Willard describes Kurtz as "broken", and his own face is obscured in darkness. Then, Kurtz's silhouette emerges into the room and he walks towards Willard. He tells Willard that they have seen the same horrors - and that Willard has the right to kill him but no right to judge him. Kurtz's words continue over the darkness and then he comes into a close-up, lit with extreme contrast where only half his face is visible. He speaks about horror and moral terror as either friends or enemies. In Willard's alternating close-up, Lance is visible in the background, spaced out and doing some kind of Tai-Chi.

Kurtz tells Willard a story of when he was with the Special Forces and they went into a camp to inoculate children and after they left, some of the adult men in the camp hacked off each inoculated child's arm. He describes weeping and breaking down, and Willard just listens. Kurtz says he never wants to forget that feeling - a mixture of shock and admiration that the Viet Cong had the strength to do that, simply in the name of the fight. Judgement, he says, is "not what defeats us." Then, as if he has already accepted his fate, Kurtz tells Willard that if he is to be killed, someone should go to his home and tell his son everything about his father. Willard examines his hand, stretching his fingers.

The final sequence of the film has few words - the catharsis of Willard's journey is almost entirely experiential for the audience. Kurtz stands in the doorway of the temple as a few men lead a water buffalo down the stairs towards a bonfire where the residents of the compound have gathered. They are preparing for a ceremonial sacrifice - there is dancing and music and rain. A man dances around the water buffalo with a ladle of water. Lance, surrounded by children, drinks rice wine out of a mug. The men dance with shields and spears, and women hold chickens upside down.

Cut to the PBR where Willard is lying on the floor, brandishing a long knife. A voice from Trang calls out from the radio, but he ignores it. In his voice-over, Willard reflects that he will likely be made a major for killing Kurtz - and yet, this is what Kurtz himself wants most of all. He wants Willard to take his pain away, to die like a soldier and not a renegade. Willard climbs out of the boat on his hands and knees and dives into the river.

Cut to a close-up of the murky river with a coating of mist swirling over it. Willard's painted head rises out of it, his paranoid eyes darting around. Meanwhile, on shore, it is raining, torches are lit, and people are dancing. Kurtz retreats into the temple for the last time. The song "This is The End" by The Doors starts to play as Willard creeps into the temple, crouched like an animal. Kurtz sits at the end of the hallway, waiting. Outside, the men start hacking at the water buffalo with machetes, and its reddish innards ooze onto the ground. Kurtz speaks into his recorder when he sees Willard coming towards him. As Willard's blade comes down onto Kurtz, the machetes continue to slice into the water buffalo until it crumples to the ground. In soft focus, Willard, bare-chested, completes his mission successfully. Cut to a close-up of Kurtz's bloodied profile as he lies on the ground. He whispers his dying words, "The horror...the horror."

In a low angle shot, Willard emerges into Kurtz's sleeping chambers. He finds a typewriter and a stack of typed pages - Kurtz's writings. A close-up draws attention to the red scrawl on one of the pages, which reads, "Drop the Bomb, Exterminate them all!" For a moment, Willard sits at the typewriter. Then, he looks outside and sees that all the people have gathered at the doorway. He takes the manuscript and comes outside, revealing the crowd in a point-of-view shot. Everyone kneels before Willard. In a close-up, Willard turns his head towards the darkness.

He slowly descends the temple stairs and drops his bloody knife. In a high angle wide shot, the people part and allow Willard to walk through the crowd. Everything is silent and still. Willard takes Lance's hand and leads him towards the shore. Dissolve to Willard and Lance back on the boat and the people collected on the stairs, watching them go. The radio starts buzzing with voices, and Willard turns it off. In the final shot of the film, Willard's face is layered on top of images from Kurtz's compound and the helicopters. The words, "the horror... the horror" repeat, and the rain comes down harder. Fade to black.

Analysis

When Willard is finally granted audience with Kurtz, the film quickly changes in pace and the structure loosens, which was not as much of an intentional choice but rather Coppola's creative way to resurrect the story after a problematic shoot. Coppola shot these final scenes in the second phase of production, post-hurricane, while still struggling to figure out how to conclude his massive epic. To further complicate matters, when Marlon Brando arrived in the Philippines, he was extremely overweight and acutely self-conscious about it. The legendary actor was demanding, but also completely unprepared. For this reason, the character of Kurtz evolved during the shoot, slowing things down considerably.

The first major decision came out of necessity: Vittorio Storaro developed a lighting concept to conceal Brando's girth, "creating a black shadow so that bits of [Kurtz] can emerge, like truth emerging from matter" (Cowie 80). The effect is ultimately transcendent and creepy, setting the ethereal tone for the conclusion of Willard's journey. However, Coppola could not stage his intended ending with his oversized Kurtz, so he was forced to re-tool his plan. It just so happened that Eleanor Coppola was filming her documentary footage on a day off and stumbled upon the Ifugao extras performing a ritual water buffalo slaughter. She ran to get her husband, and decided to incorporate it into the final scene, intercut with Willard's slaughter of Kurtz.

The confrontation between Willard and Kurtz is emotionally stripped-down, taking away any pretenses. The famous shot of Willard's head rising out of the murky water is symbolic of his reversion to his animalistic impulses. Additionally, Willard's wet hair and painted face make him look more and more like Kurtz. Willard and Kurtz have shared many of the same experiences. In Willard's initial briefing, we learn that he has taken on these kinds of highly classified missions for the C.I.A. before - murder in the name of patriotism. We witness his "complicity in the madness of war" become sealed when he murders the wounded Vietnamese woman on the sampan (Cowie 159). However, Willard cannot succumb to the darkness in his heart and chooses to refuse Kurtz's throne.

Likewise, Kurtz had performed risky missions as part of the Army before he went rogue. Even before the full-scale military mobilization in Vietnam, it was common for Green Berets to "operate covertly on the fringes of battle. They often ignore[d] the normal rules of war in their day to day battles in isolated areas" (Cowie 141). Kurtz had "gotten off the boat" before, when he undertook Operation Arcangel without clearance. Instead of being disciplined, though, the media forced the Army's hand, and he was promoted. This time, though, Kurtz had gone too far; furthermore, his actions do not help the American cause. The duties he carried out as a respected member of the American mission have, in turn, transformed Kurtz into a major threat against American colonial power.

Kurtz's operation in Cambodia places him squarely out of the American grasp, both literally and figuratively. Cambodia was officially off-limits to American intervention, which is why Willard's crew is so apprehensive about going there. However, during the Vietnam War, there were reports of B-52 attacks over the border in Cambodia, especially after the Tet Offensive. In this way, Coppola draws attention to the American tactic of pushing the envelope further and further in a desperate attempt to win an impossible war instead of taking a moment to reflect on the emotional and physical toll of the conflict. Derek Malcolm wrote in *The Guardian*, "Kurtz's career must be terminated with extreme prejudice, as if the military-industrial complex responsible for the hostilities were some sort of Godfather-like Mafia sending a hitman to deal with a disloyal capo."

Willard's time at Kurtz's compound proves that the man is, indeed, fighting his own war. His followers are the Montagnards, ethnic Cambodians living in Vietnam. (In the film, the Montagnards are played by Ifugao extras from the North Philippines). During the Vietnam War, the US Special Forces (and the CIA) would recruit Montagnards as covert troops to help monitor VC infiltration across the border between South Vietnam and Cambodia. Green Berets encouraged their Montagnard fighters to commit atrocities, and many of the Montagnards found this newfound position to be demoralizing. According to Coppola, the Montagnards "were not savage peoples, but they were primitive peoples..." He saw Kurtz as "a kind of Margaret Mead who hasn't really gone native but respects the native customs" (Cowie 27). It is a contradiction, though, to see Kurtz preaching about morality and psychology while his front steps are strewn with human heads. He has convinced himself that his actions are necessary in order to halt the spread of American evil, which parallels American Cold War philosophy: Stop the spread of communism at any cost.

Through the character of Captain Colby, Coppola shows his audience that the dark desire to cross into the jungle is not just isolated within Kurtz, but that it threatens every person. This darkness is inside Willard, too, but in order to reject it, he must stare it right in the eye and choose to vanquish it. In this way, Coppola crafts Willard as a subjective character, a symbol for America in Vietnam. Kurtz, like the war, gets out of control, and in order to control the fallout, Willard, like the Americans, must accept the corrosion of morality that motivated the conflict in the first place. Unlike Kurtz, though, Willard chooses to walk away and fulfill his new mission: to share Kurtz's story with his son back home, and maybe one day, Kurtz's horrible legacy can be used to prevent another Vietnam.

Suggested Essay Questions

1. **Willard comments that he had been back home, only to find that it doesn't exist anymore. What does this say about his character? Why is he back in Vietnam?**

   Willard has returned to Vietnam because his first tour has unsettled him. In order to conquer the demons that are eating away at him, he must come face to face with his internal darkness and choose to reject it. The Vietnam War toppled the post World War II American mentality of a soldier as a hero. WWII was painted as a clear conflict between good and evil, and the allies were perceived as unequivocally good. With only a vague understanding of the cause, the Vietnam War spiraled out of control. The line between patriotism and brutality became increasingly blurry, and many American soldiers could not grasp their mission on an ideological level. Many of them committed terrible atrocities in the name of patriotism (like Willard and Mr. Clean murdering the innocent Vietnamese people on the sampan). Back home, though, many returning soldiers felt lost, confused, and depressed. Willard deals with the alienation by returning to the only place where he feels like he is useful.
2. **After meeting the roguish Kilgore, Willard wonders what the US Army has against Kurtz. Compare the characters of Kurtz and Kilgore and the roles they play in the war. Why does one pose a threat to the American efforts in Vietnam?**

   Kilgore is an archetype of American jingoism, the film's John Wayne character. His character is, on one hand, completely absurd (i.e. insisting that his men go surf while there is a battle raging on the shore). In a way, Kilgore is also fighting his own war, just like Kurtz. He is uninterested in his supposed assignment to escort Willard and his men to Vin Din Drop until he learns that it's a great place to surf; he is eking out a way of life in the midst of insanity. Meanwhile, Kurtz is living over the Cambodian border, preaching about the horror the Americans have perpetrated in Vietnam. Still, there are dead bodies hanging all over his compound, which, as the Photojournalist explains, are the result of Kurtz's tendency to "go too far." Despite the similarities in their methods, Kilgore still has his eye on American victory, no matter how skewed his definition of the word. Kurtz, on the other hand, has the opposite goal, and therefore - must be silenced.
3. **Describe Coppola's use of darkness and shadows, especially in Kurtz's compound. How does the extreme lighting enhance the story? How?**

   The theme of light vs. darkness is at the core of Joseph Conrad's *Heart of Darkness*, so it is fitting that Coppola would utilize this contrast while telling the story of Willard and Kurtz. Coppola and Vittorio Storaro came up with a concept to reveal Kurtz in pieces, tiny slices of illumination cutting through the darkness, which is a subjective choice and aligns the viewer with Willard. At the beginning of Willard's journey, he (and the audience) believes that Kurtz is insane. However, as we travel further up the river and recognize the breadth of the destruction, both physical and moral, that has resulted from America's campaign in Vietnam, it is possible to understand how a man like Kurtz might snap. By the time Willard arrives at Kurtz's compound, Kurtz does not seem insane, rather, he is completely lucid about the darkness inside himself. Willard also has demons inside of him, and the only way for him to vanquish them is to face his internal darkness head on. The lighting in this scene is demonstrative of this struggle, though as its invention was one of necessity. Coppola and his cinematographer lit this scene to disguise Brando's girth, but in the process created an indelible and celebrated image.

4. **Why does Chief try to strangle Willard before his death? What does this say about both of their characters and how they are choosing to fight this war?**

   At the beginning of their journey, Chief seems to be a serious, by-the-books military man. He performs his duty diligently, but there is something unapproachable and mysterious about him. He does not speak forlornly of home in the way the other crew members do. He is steely and determined, and the primary opponent against Willard's unorthodox mission into Cambodia. After he witnesses Willard shoot the wounded Vietnamese woman in cold blood instead of taking her to safety, he truly realizes the nature of this journey. However, Chief is the one who opens fire on the Montagnard attackers, leading to his death. He tries to strangle Willard because he believes that he is responsible for dragging the PBR crew into this terrible situation. It is a last gasp effort to rail against the system.

5. **Examine Coppola's depiction of the psychedelic drug culture in *Apocalypse Now*, especially in the characters of Lance and Chef.**

   The drug culture that was rampant in America came with the country's youth into Vietnam. In *Apocalypse Now*, it's mostly a way for soldiers like Chef and Lance to stay numb from what's happening around them. For Lance, constantly being high allows him to maintain his childlike innocence. For example, he is able to distance himself from Mr. Clean's death, and only worries about his puppy. He uses a purple signal flare, which is supposed to be used for alerting others to trouble, as a way to create a "purple haze" (a Jimi Hendrix song as well as slang for LSD). Chef, on the other hand, "resents the mission and turns to dope by way of consolation" (Cowie 167).

6. **Why do you think Mr. Clean kills the people on the sampan before knowing whether or not they are dangerous? What does this scene say about the American effort in Vietnam?**

Mr. Clean is extremely young, and represents a lot of the Americans that went to Vietnam. The average age of the American soldier was only 19. A lot of these young men and women were unclear about why they were in Vietnam and what they were fighting for, and they were terribly impressionable. Coppola fashioned the sampan massacre after the My Lai Massacre, a much larger-scale slaughter of innocent people. Many of the soldiers who were involved in My Lai described just being completely out of control. Because the "enemy" was so elusive (the Viet Cong were experts in guerilla warfare) and military intelligence was often unreliable, many innocent Vietnamese people died.

7. **Describe the different journeys in *Apocalypse Now*, both literal and figurative.**

   Willard goes on a literal journey throughout *Apocalypse Now*. At the beginning of the film, he is a broken man. He has seen some things during his first tour of Vietnam that he cannot forget, and done things in the name of patriotism that he cannot face. His journey to find Kurtz is the catalyst for Willard's own journey of self-discovery - he must dig into the depths of his soul and face his internal darkness, embodied by Kurtz, and then decide either to succumb to it or vanquish it. The physical journey is the PBR's voyage up the Nung River to find Kurtz. The mission has many casualties, including three crew members and thousands of Vietnamese civilians, as the PBR ventures deeper into the jungle. Only Willard and Lance survive, and both of them are eternally transformed.
8. **The sequence at the Do Lung Bridge embodies, in many ways, Coppola and Milius' ideology about the war. Describe how this point in Willard's journey is a microcosm of the war at large.**

   The environment around the Do Lung Bridge is completely chaotic. There does not seem to be anyone in charge when Willard asks around. As Chief describes, "We [The Americans] build it every night, Charlie blows it right back up again. Just so the Generals can say the road's open' (Cowie 168). It's emblematic of the war because even though the administration was eager to sell the importance of the war to the public, the soldiers on the ground were locked into this kind of futile exercise every day. The Sisyphean task of rebuilding a bridge only to see it blown up again is an expression of madness. The army, at this point, was decapitated, and had no strong moral center. The scene at the Do Lung Bridge really encapsulates this chaos.
9. **There are very few Vietnamese characters in *Apocalypse Now* who are distinct or actually have speaking roles. What does this say about Coppola's point of view about the war?**

   Historians have often cited the guerilla skills of the Viet Cong as one of the reasons for the American capitulation in Vietnam. By choosing not to show the enemy, Coppola takes the audience into the American point of view. For example, at Do Lung Bridge, the soldiers hear "Charlie," who are using American slang in order to taunt their opponents. They literally have no idea who they are firing at. Generals like Kilgore saw nothing of taking out entire villages - the innocent lives meant nothing as long as they got to "smell victory." In this way, Coppola frames the American lies, not the Viet Cong, as the clear antagonists of *Apocalypse Now*.

10. **Scholars and critics (and Francis Ford Coppola himself) have often compared the production of *Apocalypse Now* to the Vietnam War itself. What are the similarities between the two?**

    Francis Ford Coppola's wife, Eleanor, kept a detailed diary during the production of *Apocalypse Now*. She famously wrote: "More and more it seems like there are parallels between the character of Kurtz and Francis. There is the exhilaration of power in the face of losing everything, like the excitement of war when one kills and takes the chance of being killed" (Cowie 123). By this point in the production process, Coppola was behaving like a megalomaniac, but underneath, he was terrified that the film was going to be an epic failure as everything spiraled out of control. Meanwhile, during the Vietnam War, the American administration kept pushing forward, desperate to keep the citizens at home supporting an increasingly messy war effort. Media manipulation had a major effect on public perception, which Coppola indicates with his cameo as part of a newsreel crew, "directing" Willard to "just go through, like you're fighting! Don't look in the camera!" as he arrives at Vin Din Drop. Offset, Coppola had to keep the drama away from the media, too. During production, United Artists "sent a memo to the actors asking them not to give interviews, and that Gerald Rafshoon and Patrick Cadell, the Atlanta-based advertising team that handled President Carter's campaign, would be handling the picture and that all statements must first be checked by them and United Artists" (Higham). A film about a war waged in chaos and confusion was plagued by similar (though obviously lower-stake) problems.

The Vietnam War

Though France had started to invade Indochina in the mid 1850s, by the middle of the 19th Century, the Vietnamese Resistance had become a serious threat to the colonial power structure. In 1883, France imposed a 'protectorate' on Vietnam, but ended up losing nearly 50,000 troops to the cause by the end of World War II. In the United States, the Truman Administration recognized the importance of maintaining France as an ally, and decided to support the French effort in Indochina. Despite the influx of American dollars, though, the French troops were forced to surrender to North Vietnamese Communist forces at Dien Bien Phu on May 7, 1954.

In the early 1960s, the Saigon government was not faring much better against the North Vietnamese Communists. At the time, General Maxwell Taylor, a Korean War veteran, was President Kennedy's Chairman of the Joint Chiefs of staff and his closest military advisor. Taylor told Kennedy that losing Vietnam to communist control would put the entire region in jeopardy (Cowie 141). Kennedy, meanwhile, was interested in building up the presence of Green Berets in Vietnam. These special forces were trained in guerilla warfare, and often used questionable tactics, believing that their missions were the key to maintaining the American way of life and suppressing the Communist threat. (The fictional Kurtz was modeled after these soldiers.) They also tended to operate outside the normal confines of diplomacy. However, Kennedy was reluctant to unleash a full-on deployment of American troops.

After Kennedy's untimely death, Lyndon B. Johnson took over the Oval Office. America continued to support Saigon with military advisors and huge amounts of money, but it soon became clear that the ARVN were out-maneuvered against the Viet Cong. President Johnson felt that he had no choice - he could either deploy American Combat troops into Vietnam or watch the entire region fall into communist hands.

Nobody could have predicted the disastrous outcome of the mobilization. After all, it was the height of the Cold War, shortly after the Cuban Missile Crisis, and the American psyche was generally healthy after the Allies' resounding victory during World War II. Although World War II had certainly taken a major toll on the American population and resources, the public saw it as "A war which had climaxed with the GIs feted as they liberated the capitals of Europe, and with the unforgettable rapture of the victory parades, was immortalized in movies as yet another step towards America's manifest destiny" (Bilton & Sim, 27).

However, despite the American military's prediction that the Viet Cong would back down from the first glimpse of the American military machine, the VC's style of guerilla warfare kept them at arm's length from all of America's high-tech killing tools. Military commanders could not *find* their enemy most of the time, much less vanquish the entire movement.

By 1967, "more than a million tons of supplies a month were flowing into Vietnam to maintain the US military presence" (Cowie 142). Major press manipulation was crucial in allowing the American administration to maintain support for the war at home, which was quickly falling apart. In January of 1968, both North and South Vietnam announced a 2-day ceasefire because of the Tet Lunar New Year celebrations. However, on January 30th, the first day of the Tet ceasefire, the Communists launched a major well-coordinated attack, with more than 80,000 troops attacking more than 100 towns and cities. The Tet Offensive was the largest military operation that had occurred on either side by that point in the war, and had a profound effect on the American morale, both on the ground and at home. It became clear that the military presence in Vietnam was having little to no effect, and the nation became completely polarized over it.

After the My Lai Massacre, when American soldiers killed more than 500 innocent civilians, the American public was in a state of frenzied outrage. More than 30,000 American lives had been lost, for reasons that seemed less clear day by day. Reports of outrage flooded American television screens on a daily basis. It is in this environment that John Milius and the Zoetrope team were inspired to make *Apocalypse Now*, and many of the characters and events in the film are based on real events and people.

When Nixon reached office in 1969, troops had been on the ground in Vietnam for nearly 7 years, and 300 American soldiers were dying every week. In the United States, students organized to protest drafts, burning their draft cards in demonstration on university campuses. A round of peace talks in Paris fell apart due to ongoing communist attacks in South Vietnam. Eventually, in the early 1970s, Nixon started pulling back the American military presence and the Paris Peace Accords were signed in 1973. The truce between North and South Vietnam lasted for a brief time after the American withdrawal, but the conflict flared up again and the North conquered the South in 1975.

END THE
WAR
IN
INDOCHINA
VIETNAM
NOW

Author of ClassicNote and Sources

A. Boghani, author of ClassicNote. Completed on November 21, 2013, copyright held by GradeSaver.

Updated and revised Christine McKeever December 30, 2013. Copyright held by GradeSaver.

Bilton, Michael and Kevin Sim. Four Hours in My Lai. New York City: Penguin, 1992.

Biskind, Peter. Easy Riders, Raging Bulls: How the Sex-Drugs-And-Rock n' Roll Generation Saved Hollywood. New York City: Simon & Schuster, 1998.

Cowie, Peter. Coppola: A Biography. New York City: Da Capo Press, 1994.

Cowie, Peter. The Apocalypse Now Book. New York City: First Da Capo Press, 2001.

Delorme, Stephane. Masters of Cinema: Francis Ford Coppola (Cahiers du Cinema). Paris: Cahiers du cinema Sarl, 2010.

Harmetz, Aljean. "'Apocalypse Now' to be Re-Released." The New York Times. 1987-08-20. 2013-08-02. <http://www.nytimes.com/1987/08/20/movies/apocalypse-now-to-be-re-released.html>.

Higham, Charles. "Coppola's Vietnam Movie is a Battle Royal." The New York Times. 1977-05-15. 2013-08-02. <http://query.nytimes.com/mem/archive/pdf?res=F1091EFC395516778DDDAC0994DD405

Malcolm, Derek. "Francis Ford Coppola: Apocalypse Now." The Guardian. 1999-11-30. 2013-08-02. <http://www.theguardian.com/film/1999/nov/04/josephconrad>.

Francis Ford Coppola Presents: Apocalypse Now. Dir. Francis Ford Coppola. Perf. Martin Sheen, Marlon Brando, Robert Duvall, Larry Fishburne, Dennis Hopper, Frederic Forrest, Albert Hall, Sam Bottoms. Paramount, 1979. DVD

i[Hearts of Darkness: A Filmmaker's Apocalypse]. Dir. Eleanor Coppola. ZM Productions, 1991. DVD

Essay: Rationalizing the Fear Within

by Brad Champion
November 09, 2005

Both The Things They Carried and Apocalypse Now explore the trauma of the Vietnam War and its influence on soldiers' fears. Similar characters appear in both works, their identities crafted to represent different aspects of human nature. The protagonists, Captain Willard and Tim O'Brien, tell frame stories through their own points of view, giving the audience windows to the guilt and hollowness, death and savagery rife in war-torn Vietnam. Each finds himself suffocated by guilt, choking at an explanation for the endless, meaningless death and violence. Similarly, Chef, the private on Willard's boat, and Curt Lemon of O'Brien's platoon mirror each other with their immaturity, their carefree rambunctious behavior and their gruesome, avoidable deaths. With the protagonist of each story as its guide, the audience examines the degree to which fear and primal instincts consume the soldiers in the jungle. Fear in the hearts of men grows unhindered in each work, as both Willard and O'Brien strive to tell their stories as much as to placate their own fear of guilt and responsibility as to comment on the fear of others. The two works spin strikingly similar stories of insanity, guilt, and trauma, albeit through different media.

Initially, the methods of storytelling employed by each protagonist seem to be completely dissimilar: Willard's moves with the action, a first person account of the happenings as they take place, while O'Brien's jumps around from being with the action to reflecting upon it twenty years later. However, taken from a different angle, Willard's narration shows as much reflection on events and personal emotion as O'Brien's. Both narrators are jaded by the action they have seen, displayed by the way each can instantly discern what sorts of people make his company. O'Brien analyzes each of his characters through descriptions of their belongings and habits, ultimately crafting a telling portrait of each man. Likewise, Willard introduces the crew of his ship by painting their identities with a broad brush: Lance, the young surfer, Chef, the down south saucier, etc. As they move from soldier to soldier, Willard and O'Brien create indelible images in the mind of the audience, colorful personas that command pity, sympathy, and loathing.

Both Willard and O'Brien have difficulty understanding the enemy. When reading the dossier on Kurtz, Willard's voiceover reveals his thoughts and emotions about Kurtz's life and sudden, erratic decisions; in "Ambush," O'Brien does the same when talking about the man he killed. O'Brien tries to imagine what the man's life would have been like were it not for the grenade, and even gives an objective point of view and he hypothetically tells the story to his daughter. The blend of surmise and objectivity of O'Brien's account in "Ambush" bears resemblance to Willard's interactions with Kurtz. Like O'Brien, Willard attempts to put himself in Kurtz's shoes, wondering if the thirst for action could turn him native and savage, as it did the colonel. Yet in each case, the protagonist falters when attempting to understand his enemy, and essentially makes the title "enemy" a misnomer. Illuminating one of the problems with the concept of war, both Willard and O'Brien sympathize with the men they are orders to kill and add difficulty to a simple task. The struggle to rationalize the act of killing is hardest for O'Brien, as the Vietnamese man was an innocent compared to the monster of Colonel Kurtz. Willard, on the other hand, sympathizes with Kurtz because he has taken the same path as his enemy, and feels the same potential for evil inside of himself. In both works, the frame story structure reveals the attempts of the protagonist to rationalize the horror around them.

Fear, the impetus of survival, has a pronounced role in both Apocalypse Now and The Things They Carried. Their machismo makes soldiers attempt to mask their fear, thereby allowing it to grow within them. Attempting to deny their fear makes soldiers act illogically, almost turning them "savage" in the end. As O'Brien describes in "The Dentist", Curt Lemon insists on having a perfectly good tooth pulled because he fears ridicule by his peers and superiors so deeply. He had shamed himself by fainting during a routine military checkup and needed to reclaim his toughness by showing that he could withstand the pulling of a tooth, regardless of whether or not he needed that tooth to be pulled. Similarly, Lemon's last action - playing catch with a hand grenade - illustrates the juxtaposition of war and camaraderie, the morbid fun in which the soldiers engage to sustain an illusion of safety.

Just as Lemon's inherent fear causes him to behave in insane ways, so does that of Chef, the saucier onboard Willard's boat. Chef's death at the hands of Kurtz's savages takes place off screen, leading to a scene depicting his mangled corpse. Like Lemon's death, Chef's is brief and gruesome, and overshadows the rest of his life. Prior to his gruesome exit, Chef loses touch with reality on the river when he decides to look for fruit in the jungle. As Chef and Willard run off into enemy territory, risking their lives only to look for mangoes, they too submit their will to the illogical judgment of fear. The fear inside them, stoked by the savage passions of the jungle and the war around them, instills and Chef and Willard the desire for safety, the need to revert to familiar surroundings to assuage the trauma of Vietnam. The jungle's wildness consumes them on this fruitless quest, and the two soldiers flee from a tiger. The tiger, like the grenade, presents a force of reckoning to the men. It destroys the illusion of safety created by temporary peace, the lull between bouts of combat. The tiger throws Chef and Willard back into ugly reality, and the men forget their mangoes back on the Me-Kong. Their fears, and those of all soldiers, eventually come down to one thing - the fear of death.

As their fears deepen in the forests of Vietnam, all the man become less human. In O'Brien's stories, ignorant actions reveal the savage nature some of the men have developed. Kiley blows his own toe off to get out of action, for instance, and Lee Strunk begs Jensen to spare his life regardless of their pact. Apocalypse Now delves much further into the evolution of fear, as Kurtz represents an embodiment of fear itself. Once an eloquent, highly respected war hero, Colonel Kurtz devolves into a mind irreparably twisted and contorted by fear and evil. Kurtz's evil forces Willard to consider whether he himself has the capacity for the same. Though O'Brien's stories posses nothing as cohesive as the fear consolidated in Kurtz, many of their characters embody similar traits. Azar, for example, exudes wholly mercenary qualities throughout much of his time, showing blatant disregard for the value of life before showing deference to Kiowa's memory.

In the end, both mental and physical survival depends on soldiers' ability to sort out his fears. O'Brien does this via his writing, feeling that preserving the memories of fallen friends can alleviate his guilt. Willard, however, submits to his fears, fulfilling his duty and slaying the evil Kurtz. Exiting the colonel's temple shirtless and sweating, chest heaving in the heat of the jungle and wild eyes flashing upon legions of native people, he resembles an idol. As he mutters the same last words Kurtz did - "The horror" - Willard shows how the experience has changed him. While O'Brien exorcized his fears by writing about them, Willard's clearly remain.

The war itself deserves credit for any similarities between these two works. War, as an institution, commands men to act against their nature. Men are not supposed to kill each other for reasons unknown, blow off their own toes to escape confrontation, or rip out their own good teeth. They are not supposed to mount severed human heads on posts or decimate a village so one man can surf. War makes them do these things. Apocalypse Now and The Things They Carried look closely at how war contorts the mind of a soldier, amplifying his fears into insanity. Using similar characters and techniques, each work produces a unique image of what war did to soldiers in Vietnam.

Quiz 1

1. **At the beginning of the film, how many tours of Vietnam has Capt. Willard completed?**
   A. 0
   B. 1
   C. 2
   D. 3

2. **When the two soldiers arrive at Willard's Saigon hotel room, what does he think they are there for?**
   A. To give him food
   B. To give him a Medal of Honor
   C. To institutionalize him
   D. To arrest him

3. **What is Willard wearing when the soldiers arrive to take him to headquarters for the first time?**
   A. A dress
   B. A heavy wool sweater
   C. Nothing
   D. His uniform

4. **According to Willard, where does he frequently think he is when he wakes up?**
   A. Back in America
   B. In the Oval Office
   C. In World War II
   D. In the jungle

5. **What is the name of the band who performs the iconic opening song, "This is the End"?**
   A. The Doors
   B. The Beatles
   C. The Rolling Stones
   D. The Who

6. **Why is Kurtz going to be arrested for murder?**
   A. He ordered the execution of a Cambodian film crew
   B. He killed one of his fellow soldiers
   C. He murdered an entire village of people in cold blood
   D. He ordered the execution of Vietnamese intelligence agents

7. **Why do Willard and his crew require an escort to get into the Nung River?**
   A. Because Kurtz has stationed his minions up and down the river
   B. Because there are Viet Cong all over the entries to the river
   C. Because the water is too shallow
   D. Because the river is littered with deadly crocodiles

8. **What is Lance Johnson famous for?**
   A. His good looks
   B. His hand-knife skills
   C. Surfing
   D. Waterskiing

9. **Which of the following is NOT one of Kurtz's qualifications?**
   A. He got a Masters from Harvard
   B. He attended West Point
   C. He fought in Korea
   D. He was a Rabbi in Jerusalem

10. **According to Kurtz's dossier, when did he start to behave strangely?**
   A. After his father died
   B. After he returned from Korea
   C. After his first tour of Vietnam
   D. After Lyndon Johnson took office

11. **To what does Willard compare charging men with murder in Vietnam?**
   A. Handing out speeding tickets at the Indy 500
   B. Handing out whiskey at church
   C. Handing out broccoli to vegetarians
   D. Handing out cigarettes to a chain gang

12. **Why is Willard going on his mission in a Navy PBR?**
   A. It allows him to be inconspicious
   B. It's Willard's favorite kind of boat
   C. Chief is the only commander who will take Willard
   D. It is the only boat that will go up the Nung River

13. **How does Kilgore respond when Willard first approaches him about the mission?**
    A. He starts singing "Can't Get No...Satisfaction"
    B. He gets excited to go up the Nung River
    C. He claims he hasn't heard of the mission
    D. He asks Willard to help him toss out "Death Cards"

14. **What is the purpose of putting playing cards on Vietnamese corpses?**
    A. To help family members find their loved ones
    B. To help the medics identify anyone who might be alive
    C. To let the Viet Cong know who killed them
    D. To count the number of casualties

15. **Where is Mr. Clean from?**
    A. Staten Island
    B. The South Bronx
    C. Brooklyn
    D. Flushing, Queens

16. **What country is Walter Kurtz in?**
    A. Vietnam
    B. Cambodia
    C. India
    D. Burma

17. **Which of the following is NOT a quote from Kurtz's tapes?**
    A. "What do you call it when assassins accuse the assassin?"
    B. "I will survive because of those who keep me alive"
    C. "I watched a snail crawl along the edge of a straight razor"
    D. "We have to be merciful to those who lie"

18. **What initially frustrates Willard about the crew on his boat?**
    A. He thinks they are too young to be helpful
    B. He thinks they might try to kill him
    C. He usually works alone
    D. He doesn't like any of them

19. **Where is Chef from?**
    A. St. Louis
    B. Houston
    C. New Orleans
    D. Montgomery

20. **Why do Kilgore's men sit on their helmets when preparing for an attack?**
    A. It makes the landing easier
    B. They like the thrill of it
    C. So their balls don't get blown off
    D. It's a superstition

21. **What piece of music does Kilgore use to scare victims during an airborne attack?**
    A. The Rolling Stones' Can't Get No Satisfaction
    B. Wagner's Ride of the Valkyries
    C. Handel's Messiah
    D. Beethoven's 9th Symphony

22. **How does Kilgore transport Willard's PBR to the entry point of the Nung River?**
    A. He drags it underwater
    B. He disassembles it and brings it in his helicopter
    C. He has it airlifted
    D. He says he'll get them a new boat on the other side

23. **What is Chef's culinary specialty?**
    A. Sauces
    B. Desserts
    C. Sushi
    D. Stews

24. **What does Captain Kilgore love to smell in the morning?**
    A. Napalm
    B. Fresh ocean water
    C. Cigarettes
    D. Coffee

25. **What is the motto that Kilgore has painted on his helicopter?**
   A. "Death from Above"
   B. "Down with Charlie"
   C. "Someday, This War's Gonna End"
   D. "Surf or Fight"

Quiz 1 Answer Key

1. **(B)** 1
2. **(D)** To arrest him
3. **(C)** Nothing
4. **(D)** In the jungle
5. **(A)** The Doors
6. **(D)** He ordered the execution of Vietnamese intelligence agents
7. **(B)** Because there are Viet Cong all over the entries to the river
8. **(C)** Surfing
9. **(D)** He was a Rabbi in Jerusalem
10. **(C)** After his first tour of Vietnam
11. **(A)** Handing out speeding tickets at the Indy 500
12. **(A)** It allows him to be inconspicious
13. **(C)** He claims he hasn't heard of the mission
14. **(C)** To let the Viet Cong know who killed them
15. **(B)** The South Bronx
16. **(B)** Cambodia
17. **(B)** "I will survive because of those who keep me alive"
18. **(C)** He usually works alone
19. **(C)** New Orleans
20. **(C)** So their balls don't get blown off
21. **(B)** Wagner's Ride of the Valkyries
22. **(C)** He has it airlifted
23. **(A)** Sauces
24. **(A)** Napalm
25. **(A)** "Death from Above"

Quiz 2

1. **What is Chef looking for when he goes off into the jungle while stoned?**
    A. Mangoes
    B. Avocados
    C. Sugarcane
    D. Quail

2. **What does Kilgore bring in for the "beach party"?**
    A. Beer and T-bone steaks
    B. Marijuana and prostitutes
    C. Playboy Bunnies
    D. Pizza and merlot

3. **Why does Kilgore order the napalm attack?**
    A. He is concerned that the whole village is Viet Cong
    B. He has had a psychotic break and doesn't know what he's doing
    C. He wants to make the beach safe to surf
    D. He worries that his men are outnumbered and in danger

4. **When Willard and Chef go into the woods looking for fruit, what do they find?**
    A. A tiger
    B. A Viet Cong graveyard
    C. Col. Kurtz
    D. A lost little girl

5. **What does Chef keep repeating after nearly being attacked in the woods?**
    A. "The horror, the horror"
    B. "I want to go home"
    C. "Don't get out of the boat"
    D. "I love you, Eva!"

6. **How old was Kurtz when he joined the Green Berets?**
    A. 18
    B. 28
    C. 38
    D. 48

7. **Why did Kurtz nearly get sacked for Operation Arcangel?**
   A. Because the operation was a failure
   B. Because he had no official clearance to do it
   C. Because he gave away valuable intelligence
   D. Because he killed an American soldier

8. **What creates the orange smoke?**
   A. Napalm
   B. Hydrogen bombs
   C. Grenades
   D. Machine guns

9. **Why does the Sergeant at the Supply Desk refuse to give Mr. Clean fuel?**
   A. He thinks that Clean is a spy
   B. Mr. Clean doesn't know his destination
   C. He doesn't want to
   D. There is no fuel left

10. **Which crew member describes the garish stage setup as "bizarre"?**
   A. Mr. Clean
   B. Willard
   C. Phillips
   D. Chef

11. **What kind of costume is the Playmate of the Year wearing?**
   A. Hippie
   B. Soldier
   C. Cowgirl
   D. French maid

12. **What is Mr. Clean's habit that annoys Willard?**
   A. Mooning passing boats
   B. Drumming on everything
   C. Eating all the food
   D. Singing along to the radio

13. **According to Willard, what are the only two ways Charlie will be able to get home?**
    A. Death or divine intervention
    B. Death or victory
    C. Being killed or killing himself
    D. Victory or suicide

14. **How do the Playboy Bunnies travel to Hau Phat?**
    A. By boat
    B. By private Jet
    C. By helicopter
    D. By limousine from Saigon

15. **Who did Kurtz write a letter to claiming that the charges against him are "insane"?**
    A. Richard Nixon
    B. His son
    C. General Corman
    D. His wife

16. **Which crew member is responsible for massacring the Vietnamese people on the sampan?**
    A. Chef
    B. Chief
    C. Clean
    D. Lance

17. **Why is Lance behaving strangely when he goes to shore with Willard near the Do Lung Bridge?**
    A. He has amnesia
    B. He is trying to escape
    C. He has dropped acid
    D. He is sleep-deprived

18. **Why does Chief insist that Chef raid the sampan?**
    A. Because he thinks Kurtz might be hiding on board
    B. Because he wants to take their food
    C. Because he wants to see if he can steal fuel
    D. Because it could be trafficking supplies to Charlie

19. **Which of Willard's crew is a stickler for protocol?**
    A. Chef
    B. Chief
    C. Lance
    D. Clean

20. **Who is the youngest crew member on the PBR?**
    A. Willard
    B. Chief
    C. Clean
    D. Lance

21. **How long has Clean been on the PBR?**
    A. 7 months
    B. 6 days
    C. 3 weeks
    D. 2 years

22. **Which crew member does not want to help the injured Vietnamese girl on the sampan?**
    A. Mr. Clean
    B. Willard
    C. Chef
    D. Chief

23. **What does Lance keep from the sampan massacre?**
    A. A puppy
    B. A kitten
    C. Artillery
    D. A bag of rice

24. **Why does Willard get off the PBR at the Do Lung Bridge?**
    A. He needs to stretch his legs
    B. He is having hallucinations
    C. He thinks Kurtz might be there
    D. He is looking for a C.O.

25. **What does Willard do that makes his crew think differently about him?**

A. He shoots a hole in another PBR

B. He kills the Vietnamese girl's puppy

C. He kills the wounded Vietnamese girl on the sampan

D. He laughs at the Playboy Bunnies

Quiz 2 Answer Key

1. **(A)** Mangoes
2. **(A)** Beer and T-bone steaks
3. **(C)** He wants to make the beach safe to surf
4. **(A)** A tiger
5. **(C)** "Don't get out of the boat"
6. **(C)** 38
7. **(B)** Because he had no official clearance to do it
8. **(A)** Napalm
9. **(B)** Mr. Clean doesn't know his destination
10. **(A)** Mr. Clean
11. **(C)** Cowgirl
12. **(B)** Drumming on everything
13. **(B)** Death or victory
14. **(C)** By helicopter
15. **(B)** His son
16. **(C)** Clean
17. **(C)** He has dropped acid
18. **(D)** Because it could be trafficking supplies to Charlie
19. **(B)** Chief
20. **(C)** Clean
21. **(A)** 7 months
22. **(B)** Willard
23. **(A)** A puppy
24. **(D)** He is looking for a C.O.
25. **(C)** He kills the wounded Vietnamese girl on the sampan

Quiz 3

1. **Lt. Carlson describes the Do Lung Bridge as "The _______ of the world"**
    A. Armpit
    B. Beating heart
    C. Asshole
    D. Oozing wound

2. **What does Lance do to keep himself hidden from Charlie?**
    A. Hides in the belly of the boat
    B. Wears a shirt around his head
    C. Paints his face in camouflage
    D. Swims alongside the boat

3. **Who is the commanding officer at Do Lung Bridge?**
    A. There isn't one
    B. Lt. Carlson
    C. Roach
    D. Kurtz

4. **What happens at Do Lung Bridge every day?**
    A. Charlie destroys it
    B. PBRs drown beneath it
    C. American soldiers jump off it to their deaths
    D. Kurtz's men cross it

5. **What is the American soldiers' reaction with the USO Emcee first gets off the helicopter?**
    A. They storm the stage
    B. They boo
    C. They cheer happily
    D. They start singing the national anthem

6. **According to Willard, what is Charlie's idea of "R&R"?**
    A. Killing an American soldier
    B. Cold rice and a little rat meat
    C. Spying on USO shows
    D. Surfing a cool wave

7. **What do the Playboy Bunnies use as props during their performance?**
   A. American Flags
   B. Grenades
   C. Vietnamese hats
   D. Guns

8. **How does the PBR roof catch fire?**
   A. Clean fires his machine gun into it
   B. A sailor from a passing American boat throws a smoke bomb
   C. A Vietnamese fisherman throws a cigarette
   D. Chef drops a match by smoking pot

9. **Where has most of the recent intelligence about Kurtz come from?**
   A. Illegal helicopter surveillance
   B. South Korean Army spies
   C. Captured VC
   D. Kurtz's family who is trying to find him

10. **How far is Willard's destination from the Do Lung Bridge?**
   A. 25 miles
   B. 75 clicks
   C. 20 minutes
   D. 30 kilometers

11. **What happened to the last man (Capt. Colby) who undertook a mission to find Kurtz?**
   A. He went mad and killed himself
   B. Kurtz killed him
   C. He defected to Kurtz's side
   D. He's MIA

12. **What is the big news event in the newspaper that Eva sends to Chef?**
   A. The assassination of Martin Luther King, Jr.
   B. The moon landing
   C. Elvis' death
   D. The Manson Family murders

13. **What does Clean's mother send him in the mail?**
    A. A camera
    B. A tape recorder
    C. A Bible
    D. A photo album

14. **What does Lance lose during the attack that kills Mr. Clean?**
    A. His arm
    B. His gun
    C. His surfboard
    D. His puppy

15. **What state is Willard from?**
    A. Missouri
    B. Ohio
    C. Iowa
    D. Idaho

16. **What is all over the temple stairs that lead into Kurtz's chambers?**
    A. Dirty rags
    B. Human heads
    C. Human hands
    D. Feces

17. **Where is the only place that the film's title appears?**
    A. On a wall in Kurtz's compound
    B. On a destroyed helicopter at Do Lung Bridge
    C. In Kurtz's written manifesto
    D. On the mirror in Willard's Saigon hotel room

18. **What Jimi Hendrix song does Lance refer to while waving a flare around the PBR?**
    A. Foxy Lady
    B. All Along the Watchtower
    C. Purple Haze
    D. Hey Joe

19. **Which of the PBR crew members make it to Kurtz's compound?**
A. Willard, Chief, Chef
B. Willard, Lance, Chef
C. Willard, Clean, Chief
D. Willard, Lance, Clean

20. **Why did Kurtz once try to kill the Photojournalist?**
A. Because he waved an American flag
B. Because he tried to eat off Kurtz's plate
C. Because he tried to take Kurtz's picture
D. Because he woke Kurtz up from a nap

21. **What does Chief do right before he dies?**
A. He tells Lance that he's proud of him
B. He hugs Willard
C. He tries to strangle Willard
D. He tells Willard to send his tags to his family

22. **What are Chief's last words?**
A. "An Arrow"
B. "The Horror"
C. "I hate you, Willard!"
D. "A Spear"

23. **Who is the only crew member besides Willard to survive the mission?**
A. Chef
B. Chief
C. Lance
D. Clean

24. **What is the weapon that kills Chief?**
A. A spear
B. An arrow
C. A grenade
D. A gun

25. **What is Lance's drug of choice?**

A. Cocaine
B. Magic Mushrooms
C. Marijuana
D. Acid

Quiz 3 Answer Key

1. (**C**) Asshole
2. (**C**) Paints his face in camouflage
3. (**A**) There isn't one
4. (**A**) Charlie destroys it
5. (**B**) They boo
6. (**B**) Cold rice and a little rat meat
7. (**D**) Guns
8. (**B**) A sailor from a passing American boat throws a smoke bomb
9. (**C**) Captured VC
10. (**B**) 75 clicks
11. (**C**) He defected to Kurtz's side
12. (**D**) The Manson Family murders
13. (**B**) A tape recorder
14. (**D**) His puppy
15. (**B**) Ohio
16. (**B**) Human heads
17. (**A**) On a wall in Kurtz's compound
18. (**C**) Purple Haze
19. (**B**) Willard, Lance, Chef
20. (**C**) Because he tried to take Kurtz's picture
21. (**C**) He tries to strangle Willard
22. (**D**) "A Spear"
23. (**C**) Lance
24. (**A**) A spear
25. (**D**) Acid

Quiz 4

1. **Whom does Chef receive letters from while on the PBR?**
   A. His brother, Jim
   B. His son, Esposito
   C. His girlfriend, Eva
   D. His father, William

2. **What is Chef trying to do before he is killed?**
   A. Call home to say goodbye
   B. Attack Kurtz's men
   C. Pray
   D. Order an air strike on Kurtz's compound

3. **Which crew member gives Chief his "burial" at sea?**
   A. Willard
   B. Chef
   C. Lance
   D. Clean

4. **Who calls out to the crew of the PBR as they arrive at Kurtz's compound?**
   A. Captain Colby
   B. The Photojournalist
   C. Kilgore
   D. Kurtz

5. **What does Kurtz accuse Willard of being?**
   A. A simple puppet
   B. An American robot
   C. A brainless monkey
   D. An errand boy

6. **What does Willard eventually do with Kurtz's dossier?**
   A. Rips it up and throws it away
   B. Throws it in Kurtz's face
   C. Leaves it scattered around Kurtz's compound
   D. Leaves it on the PBR

7. **What does Capt. Colby say when Willard identifies him at Kurtz's compound?**
   A. He mumbles nonsense
   B. Nothing
   C. "With extreme prejudice"
   D. "The horror"

8. **What does Kurtz give to Willard while he is trapped in the bamboo cage?**
   A. The heart of a water buffalo
   B. Chef's severed head
   C. The severed head of a sheep
   D. Lance's severed head

9. **What does Willard say to Kurtz while he is trapped in the bamboo cage?**
   A. Nothing
   B. "Let me out"
   C. "I'll kill you"
   D. "You're insane"

10. **What does the Photojournalist give to Willard while he is trapped in the bamboo cage?**
    A. Water and a tab of acid
    B. Water and a cigarette
    C. Water and a chicken leg
    D. Water and a joint

11. **Complete this sentence from Capt. Colby's letter to his family: "Sell the ____, Sell the _____, Sell the _____"**
    A. Apartment, Beach House, Kids
    B. House, Car, Kids
    C. Dog, House, Kids
    D. House, Kids, Dog

12. **Which of the following is NOT one of Kurtz's possessions that Willard finds at his compound?**
    A. Photos of his family
    B. His military uniform
    C. A crucifix
    D. The Holy Bible

13. **What does Kurtz ask Willard to do for him?**
    A. Tell his son the truth
    B. Speak out against the war in Vietnam
    C. Take over the compound
    D. Kill the Photojournalist

14. **Which of the following characters does NOT have his face painted in camouflage over the course of the film?**
    A. Willard
    B. Chef
    C. Lance
    D. Kurtz

15. **What does Willard do with the knife he uses to kill Kurtz?**
    A. He throws it into the bonfire
    B. He keeps it
    C. He drops it on the ground
    D. He gives it to Lance

16. **What has Kurtz scrawled onto the typed pages of his manuscript?**
    A. "The Horror...The Horror"
    B. "Apocalypse Now"
    C. "I'm Never Coming Back"
    D. "Drop the Bomb, Exterminate them All!"

17. **In which city does Apocalypse Now begin?**
    A. Saigon
    B. Beijing
    C. Bangkok
    D. Chiangmai

18. **According to Willard's voice-over, how many missions did he complete AFTER killing Kurtz?**
    A. Hundreds
    B. One
    C. None
    D. Many

19. **What does Willard take from Kurtz's personal belongings?**
   A. His Military uniform
   B. His typed manuscript
   C. His machete
   D. His Holy Bible

20. **What is Lance doing while Willard is killing Kurtz?**
   A. Listening to the Photojournalist philosophize
   B. Trying to call Trang from the PBR
   C. Flirting with a young Cambodian woman
   D. Participating in the water buffalo sacrifice ritual

21. **What ritual is happening outside the temple while Willard murders Kurtz?**
   A. Sacrifice of a water buffalo
   B. A traditional wedding
   C. A traditional funeral
   D. Sacrifice of a goat

22. **What is dangling from a tree at Kurtz's compound when the PBR pulls up to shore?**
   A. A noose
   B. A monkey
   C. A dead body
   D. A bunch of bananas

23. **According to the Photojournalist, why are Kurtz's followers collected on the shore when the PBR arrives?**
   A. They want to escape from the compound in the boat
   B. They are hungry and want food
   C. They are afraid Willard will take Kurtz away
   D. They have heard that Lance Johnson, famous surfer, has arrived

24. **What happens to the Photojournalist at the end of the film?**
   A. He returns to the USA with Willard and Lance
   B. He accidentally drowns in the river
   C. Kurtz beheads him
   D. We don't know

25. **How many children does Col. Kurtz have?**

A. one son
B. two daughters
C. one son and one daughter
D. one daughter

Quiz 4 Answer Key

1. **(C)** His girlfriend, Eva
2. **(D)** Order an air strike on Kurtz's compound
3. **(C)** Lance
4. **(B)** The Photojournalist
5. **(D)** An errand boy
6. **(A)** Rips it up and throws it away
7. **(B)** Nothing
8. **(B)** Chef's severed head
9. **(A)** Nothing
10. **(B)** Water and a cigarette
11. **(B)** House, Car, Kids
12. **(C)** A crucifix
13. **(A)** Tell his son the truth
14. **(B)** Chef
15. **(C)** He drops it on the ground
16. **(D)** "Drop the Bomb, Exterminate them All!"
17. **(A)** Saigon
18. **(C)** None
19. **(B)** His typed manuscript
20. **(D)** Participating in the water buffalo sacrifice ritual
21. **(A)** Sacrifice of a water buffalo
22. **(C)** A dead body
23. **(C)** They are afraid Willard will take Kurtz away
24. **(D)** We don't know
25. **(A)** one son

18059174R00062

Printed in Great Britain
by Amazon